HOW TO GET AN ASBO

First published in Great Britain in 2006 by
Virgin Books Ltd
Thames Wharf Studios
Rainville Road
London
W6 9HA

A catalogue record for this book is available from the British Library.

ISBN-10 1 85227 3313
ISBN-13 9 781852273316

Designed by Virgin Books.

Printed and bound in Great Britain by MPG Books Ltd.

HOW TO GET AN ASBO

MIA WALLACE AND CLINT SPANNER

Contents

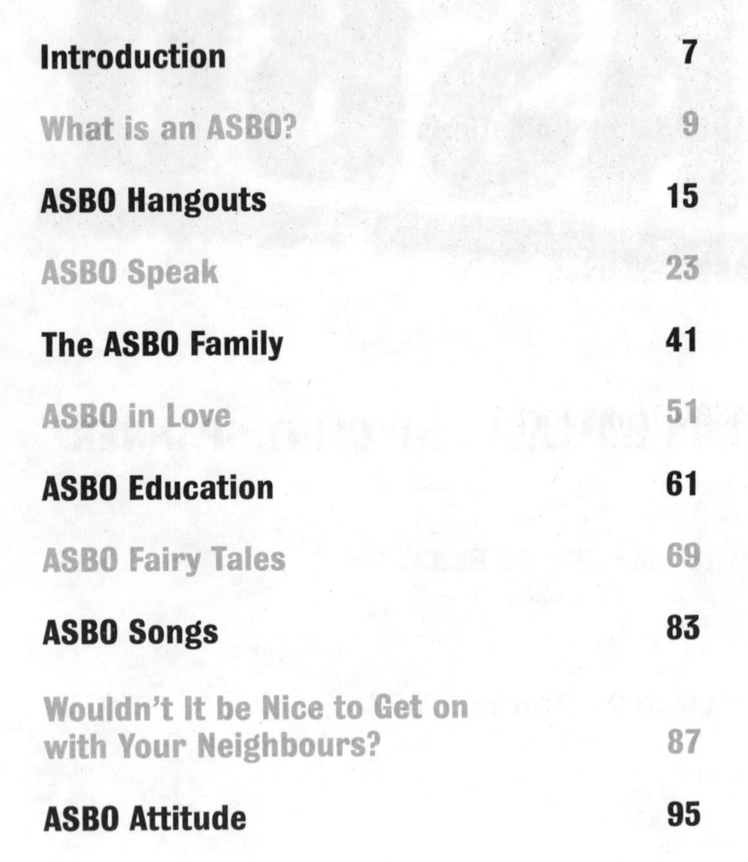

Introduction

As we all know, ASBO stands for *antisocial behaviour order*. Therefore, the best way to get one is to try doing something, anything, and then waiting for other people's reactions. For example, if you try opening a drop-in centre for kids after school in your local community, you are more likely to get an MBE. (You probably won't, but we have to take all options into consideration for this guide.) This would indeed be bad. There is nothing that can ruin street cred quite as badly as going for tea and scones at the Queen's crib.

To be certain that your behaviour is ASBO-worthy, you need to read the subtle signs from your neighbours and the general public. If they run in the other direction when they see you coming and shield small children from you, you're probably going in the right direction. Another good indication would be that you are given a nickname among the local community. Anything with the term 'Mad', 'Loony' or 'Little Bastard' as a prefix is always good.

If you have an entire family who want to join you on your ASBO quest, so much the better. ASBOs are much more fun as a game the whole family can play, and, like the Spice Girls, your community will enjoy giving varying labels to your troublesome clan. Mouthy, Tarty and Nutter will prefix well with most surnames.

Remember, age is no obstacle in the ASBO quest and the people of your local community are just as likely to report an old git sticking Post-it notes all over a car windscreen as they are a teenage boy who gets windows confused with goalposts. There are a million things that piss people off. All you have to do is find one you can do with style.

Still worried you haven't got what it takes to win the glittering prize? Want all the thrills of the dark side without leaving your bedroom? Well, never fear! With our handy How to Get an ASBO guide, you can have a go and work out some ASBO anger before you have a go at the real thing.

We would say good luck, but remember: it's all down to *bad* luck, because, if anyone asks, you didn't do anything.

What is an ASBO?

ASBO stands for Antisocial Behaviour Order. This is an order, imposed by the police, together with the local authority, on an individual who is behaving in an 'antisocial' way. ASBOs can be used in conjunction with ABCs (acceptable-behaviour contracts). The penalty for breaking an ASBO can be up to five years in prison. And, when you come out of prison, you may be lucky enough to get a CRASBO (antisocial behaviour order on conviction) which is an ASBO that can be given to you once you have been convicted of a criminal offence. The Victoria Cross of ASBOs if you like.

What is an antisocial way of behaving?

Good question. The short answer is that it varies. Anything that pisses enough people off and makes them complain about you can get you an ASBO. But, if you want a basic outline, here are the main categories as described by the government's official crime-reduction website:

- **harassment of residents or passers-by**
- **Verbal abuse**
- **Criminal damage**
- **Vandalism**
- **Noise nuisance**
- **Writing graffiti**

- Engaging in threatening behaviour in large groups
- Racial abuse
- Smoking or drinking alcohol while under age
- Substance misuse
- Joyriding
- Begging
- Prostitution
- Kerb-crawling
- Throwing missiles
- Assault
- Vehicle crime

'Nothing shady about us lot!'

Well, yes, you can do any of these things and get an ASBO, but isn't it more worthy of you creative geniuses to be inventive? If you read the official Antisocial Behaviour Act 2003, you can also find other ways of getting slapped with an ASBO, including such delights as 'Having a hedge or evergreen more than 2 meters high, that is a barrier to light'. Not much of a gardener? OK, then, how about the 'Display of advertisements in contravention of regulations' – or flyposting, as it is known to the rest of us? But these are both quite rubbish ASBOs and, if you go about boasting about how you have an ASBO because your privet is a bit overgrown, chances are you're just going to be a laughing stock.

Don't think it's only young scallies that can get an ASBO (even a crap one). In 2004 Camden Council slapped an ASBO on Sony Music for illegal flyposting that they said was costing them over £250,000 a year to clean up. However, it has also been estimated that Sony and other music companies were saving up to £8 million per year in advertising by flyposting.

All of these will give you your first rung on the ASBO ladder. But which is the one for you? As with most things, it is often better to excel at one thing than to try to spread yourself too thinly.

First you must decide how far into ASBO you wish to step.

ASBO GRADES

Grade 1 – **The Plain Silly ASBOs**. Like gardening crime and bill sticking, these are ASBOs for annoyingness. Handed out because what you've done isn't actually that bad but they can't really let you carry on, otherwise you may well end up being murdered by those you are annoying – and that is a crime. The good news is that, of course, you can never break this ASBO, and, if you did, the punishment for 'aggravated shrubbery growing' has yet to be determined under law.

GRADE
ASBO
ONE

Grade 2 – **Meat and Potatoes ASBOs**. Basically, everything you shouldn't do and would expect to get an ASBO for. Misdemeanours that are petty and annoying but not bad enough to get locked up for.

GRADE
ASBO
TWO

Grade 3 – Weird ASBOs. Weird ASBOs. The kind of thing you might do that you think is just your personal business but that caused enough annoyance to someone that they thought you should be stopped. In the bad old days, the way to do this might have been to ask you nicely. Or to try to get you some help so you wouldn't continue with such behaviour.

Luckily, we've progressed since then, and we've realised the best way to get anyone to stop doing something is to give them an ASBO, which says that they really, really can't do whatever they were trying to do and that's final. Or else.

GRADE ASBO THREE

ASBO Hangouts

it woznt me!

When it comes to getting an ASBO you will need to interact with (annoy) people you don't know. What you really covet is the hatred, fear and resentment of most people who live in your local community. But how to foster this? Well, you really need to spread your wings and get out there.

Shops

These are a fantastic place to start. Everyone has to use them and so, if you stand outside one, inevitably everyone will get to see your antics as they go in. There are two main categories: local shops and big shops. Let's start with local shops.

Local Shops – These are a great place to begin your journey to the top of the ASBO ladder. Not too far from home, they will usually be staffed by people who know or have heard of you. The first thing you will need to do is find yourself a comfortable position outside the shop. Ideally, this should be as near to the entrance as possible so that there can be no doubt that you are there.

The next step is to invite as many of your friends to join you as possible. Once there are at least six of you, two should enter the shop and make a 'purchase'. By 'purchase', what we really mean is that one of you will buy something

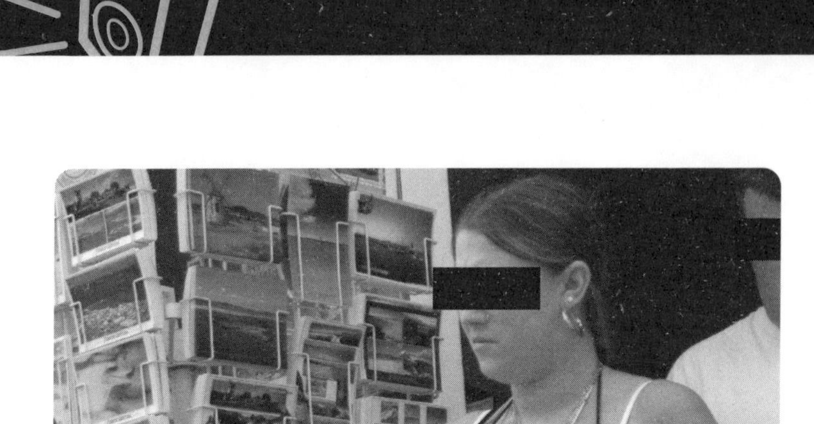

'Wish you were 'ere? I don't!'

such as a packet of Space Raiders. One by one, each of your friends can purchase items of no more than 20p each. Quickly the shopkeeper will become suspicious of your behaviour, assume you are part of a new crime wave to deplete his stash of penny chews and insist that you be on your merry way. If this cycle is repeated on a regular basis it won't be long before an ASBO follows suit.

Big Shops – These will be any of the chain stores. Possibly inside a shopping centre. While you lose the local 'community' feel that local shops have in spades, you do gain useful experience in pissing off a wider world. Big shops are also likely to be situated indoors, which is far more comfortable in inclement weather when you could spend several hours on the job. While you won't have the time to spend concentrating, in a craftsman-like manner, your efforts on one place, the opportunity to 'pick 'n' mix' your irritation levels are without limit. For example, if the clothes shop seems unusually tolerant of you, you can move on to a chemist easily. And if by some chance they all prove to be prime spots you can put in a shift at each shop (with only a small break to annoy the staff at a burger joint for lunch). Shopping centres can provide you with the chance to surprise people at places where you are likely to cause them trouble. They expect to find you flinging clothes off hangers in JJB sports but they rarely expect you to be behind them gurning in mirrors as they try on glasses in Specsavers.

Supermarkets should perhaps be mentioned in a separate paragraph. Practising annoying behaviour (using deodorant from the toiletries aisle, for example) is far easier, yet, due to the number of cameras there are, you will be picked up as acting suspiciously much more quickly. This is indeed good. Such places often have a policy of banning you

outright from ever entering one of their stores again and this is an ASBO badge of honour.

The real problem you will encounter with big shops is the fact that they are staffed by people who don't own the shop and therefore don't care too much what you do to the place, so it will be that much harder to force them to take action. The exception to this is in-store security. Their wages are not great and the job can be quite boring, so the chance to catch and arrest you may prove a highlight of the working day. Of course, you can always kick up a lot of fuss as they bring you down and tell them you know your rights.

Swing Parks – They're designed for children, yet in some areas these places have never been visited by anyone under the age of eight. It has been said that in some areas toddlers think swings are seats for smoking on and slides are something on which to build a bonfire. If you have a dog, much amusement can be had from having the barking mutt spinning round and round on a roundabout as local residents ring the RSPCA in despair.

If you have a girl/boyfriend but nowhere to go to copulate (perhaps the local bus shelter has already been trashed by a rival ASBO hunter), the swings or slide can provide almost adequate cover for all your romantic needs, while at the same time providing a public service for those of your friends who are less romantically inclined but enjoy watching.

Street Corners – A great all-purpose hangout. Unlike other hangouts, this is most fluid and without focus, and so, to provide some material to work with, we recommend that you bring something with wheels to lean on, sit in, fawn over or just prop yourself up against. It doesn't matter if it is your modded Corsa, your rusty BMX circa 1988, your pull-along shopping trolley or your baby's pram. Anything will do. It just adds to your general air of menace if you command your own chariot.

Libraries – This depends greatly on what age you are. For the younger ASBO-seeker all you can really do here is be noisy in a place where you are supposed to be quiet. But for the older person this haven of books offers a myriad possibilities. For a start, they have books that can (if you look hard enough) prove you right in any given situation. Whether it be by law, social etiquette or biblical ruling.

Also, no matter how annoying you are, unless you cause trouble and noise it is almost impossible to get thrown out of a library.

New to libraries is the Internet. This will offer a chance to look up things not in books or even to create your own website. Having your own paranoid conspiracy or complaint about the 'state of the country/parking/litter bins' website, is like a poster campaign for the twenty-first century. If you are a really cantankerous old git, the very idea that your

'Ah! Home, sweet home!'

thoughts are on the World Wide Web and can be viewed by an entire planet should prove exciting.

Local Government Offices – For the older generation, this place is like the library but with power. Contained in its chambers are people who have the power to do what you want them to. To change laws and punish wrongdoers. Sadly, in reality, they are more likely to listen to you for as long as their sanity will allow, then fob you off with excuses, promising things they'll never actually follow through with in a month of Sundays. Yes, they might well agree with you at the time that it would be a good idea to get your next-door neighbours interned on Jupiter, but don't believe them when they say they will make some calls to those higher up. Demand they do it immediately so you can hear them doing it, and when they refuse get louder and more vocal about your 'rights as a taxpayer' (although as an OAP you probably don't pay tax, but that's not the point) until they are forced to get security to escort you from the premises. This is an excellent first step in achieving an ASBO.

ASBO Speak

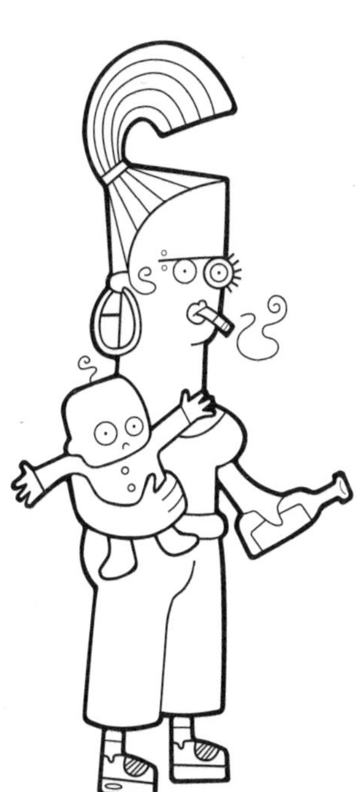

You may be able to walk the walk, but can you talk the talk? Sounding like a true menace to society is going to get you respect only from your fellow ASBO-seekers. Here we present our bespoke guide to ASBO speak. Follow the easy lessons and you'll soon be talking like a dirtbag in no time! The first thing you have to think about before you try any of the exercises is your accent. ASBO speak requires the seamless blend of your existing accent along with a good dose of 'menace'. By that we mean, for example, that, if you're from the Midlands, just imagine what 50 Cent would sound like if he came from Dudley. For the purpose of our exercises, we have adopted the most prevalent accent for ASBO speak: the mix of Estuary English with a twist.

It is essential you get the hang of replacing every vowel in a word with the 'aaagh' sound (known as the übervowel). Also, try eliminating as many consonants as possible. Let's start with some simple exercises to get warmed up:

aaahse – house
aaaht – out
abaaaht – about
caaaah – cow
daaahn – down
faaahnd – found
gaaaahn – going
maaahse – mouse
saaaah – sow
saaahnd – sound
taaahn – town
traaaht – trout

You get the idea, so let's now put some of those words together.

Aah ya gaaahn daaahn taaahn?
– Are you going to visit the town centre?

Now it's time for some of the more complex substitutions. In ASBO speak, one of the big golden rules is you never use 'th' at the start of a word, the most important example being the word 'the': it has to be replaced with 'da' – it's ASBO law. For example, 'In the hood' becomes 'In da hood'. This should give any listener the impression that you are a serious ASBO-seeker and probably listen to far too much US gangsta rap for someone who lives in a small English provincial town. The second most common substitution of 'th' is with a single or double 'f'. This substitution is often used in conjunction with the replacement of 'ing' with 'ink'. Have a go at the following examples:

fanks – thanks

fearter – theatre

fink – think

nuffink – nothing

sumffink – something

Before we move on to learn some actual phrases, we must mention the use of the Australian question intonation by many ASBO-seekers. You will find that, for no reason, a tag question is appended to every sentence, using the word 'yeah?', 'like?' or 'innit?' Some may even use a questioning phrase such as 'do ya naaah wo I mean?' In true ASBO style, this question does not require an answer. If you do confirm that you do indeed know what the ASBO-seeker meant, you are just showing your ignorance. ASBO-seekers use the question intonation only to annoy.

Let's put together what we have already learned, so you can start to sound like a true ASBO-seeker.

I'm gaaahn daaahn taaahn, yeah?
– I'm going to visit the town centre.

I daahnt naaah nuffink, abaaaht it, innit?
– I do not know anything about it.

I'm gaaahn raaahn Kev's aaahse, like?
– I'm going round to Kevin's abode.

Now you have the basic grasp of this language, it's time to practise some real phrases. We have picked some choice phrases for you to use in the street and in shops and other potential ASBO hangout places.

In the street and in shops

Diss place is safe, mate; what do ya fink?
– I rather like it here outside my local convenience store; what are your views on this matter?

it WOZnt me!

Can ya get us two packs o' skins, ten straights and some Revels, yeah?

– If you are going into the local convenience store, I would like two packets of rolling papers, ten of the store's cheapest cigarettes and a bag of Revels (just in case my cannabis smoking brings on an attack of hunger later).

Isn't dat da schlaaag Kev banged da uvver night?

– I do believe that is the woman of loose morals that Kevin copulated with the other night, unless I'm mistaken.

If he looks at me like dat again, I'm gonna faaackin' merk 'im, innit?

– If that gentleman looks at me in that aggressive manner again, I am going to fucking do him.

"

I 'ave no idea who da faaaver is: it was dark behind da chippy, like?

– I have no idea who the father of my child is: it was too dark behind the fish-and-chip shop to identify the gentleman I was copulating with clearly.

Naaah, fanks, mate, I'm gonna get some meat 'n' chips later, yeah?

– Thank you for your kind invitation of dinner at your house, but I must turn your offer down, because I'm going to purchase a delicious meal of donner kebab meat and chips for my supper.

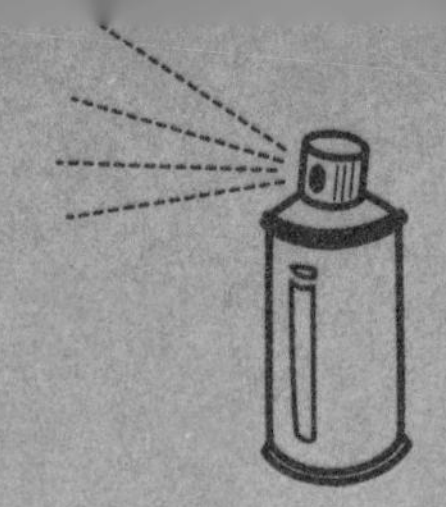

Oi, mate, can ya tell us where da paaaahnd shop is?
– Excuse me, I'm a visitor to this town, and I was wondering where I could find the famous emporium that sells every item for just one pound.

Oi mate. Can ya tell us where da post office is so I can cash me nash?
– Excuse me, I'm a visitor to this town; can you tell me where the local post office is so I can cash my giro?

Five paaahnd on dat key and two scratchies, I feelin' lucky!
– Can you credit this electricity prepayment key with five pounds – and I would also like two National Lottery scratch cards, since I believe Lady Luck is with me today!

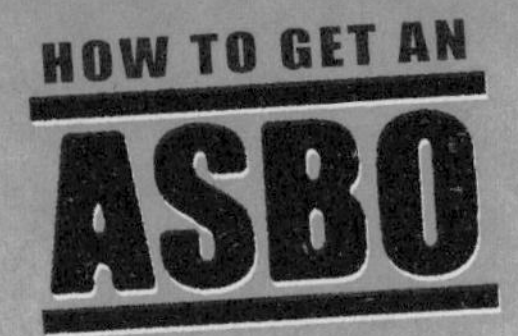

At the police station

It wasn't me, I ain't never done nuffink, yeah?
– Whatever you are thinking of accusing me of, I have not done it, since I'm completely innocent and have never committed a criminal act in my life.

'It's a fair cop, guv'

It wasn't me: I was raaahnd me mate Kev's aaaahse at da time, yeah?

– Whatever you are accusing me of, it was not I: my friend Kevin is quite happy to defend me in a court of law to provide me with an alibi.

I ain't sayin' nuffink until I've seen me brief!

– Can you please call the duty solicitor for me, as I need a legal professional.

I 'ave been fitted up, I is ganna sue da po-lice, yeah?

– I believe I have had evidence planted on me by a rogue police officer; upon my release, I am going to start immediate legal action against my local constabulary for wrongful imprisonment.

I naaah me rights, you can't do dat!
– I am hoping to convince this officer that I have read the Police and Criminal Evidence Act.

The DSS office or jobcentre

I need a loan t'get some curtains/cutlery/bed for me crib
– I need to apply for a crisis loan, as I have no money to go drinking with my friends this weekend.

I need a grant to sort me yard out, like?
– I live in private rented accommodation with a substantial garden, and I need some tools to keep the grounds in good repair.

I is disabled because of da pain in me back, can I get any more nash?
– Can I get any disability benefits on top of my job seeker's allowance, since I have a nonspecific back pain?

I is addicted to da lash. I 'erd dat ya get more dollars if you is an alky?
– I've heard a rumour among my friends and relatives that you can get more money if you can prove to a DSS doctor that you are an alcoholic.

I can't do dat job ya see, I 'ave dat fing where you jumble all da letters up, innit?
– I can't do the office job you are offering me, because I'm dyslexic.

I can't do dat job, ya see: me doc said if I get up before 9 a.m. I could 'ave a cardiac arrest, yeah?

– I can't do that job you are offering me, since it would mean getting out of bed before 9 a.m. and that would never do, since I like to spend my mornings watching *The Jeremy Kyle Show.*

I can't do dat job ya see, as I suffer from dat SAD fing, ya naaagh?

– I can't take that job you are offering me since it involves night work, and I may suffer from seasonal affective disorder.

If ya take away me nash, ma children will go 'ungry, yeah?

– My children already suffer a poor diet mainly consisting of hot dogs and economy pizza; if you withdraw my benefits they will lapse into malnutrition in a matter of days.

The nightclub

Day water daaahn da pints, get me a Hooch!

– I think this nightclub waters down its draught beers; can you please purchase me a bottled alcopop.

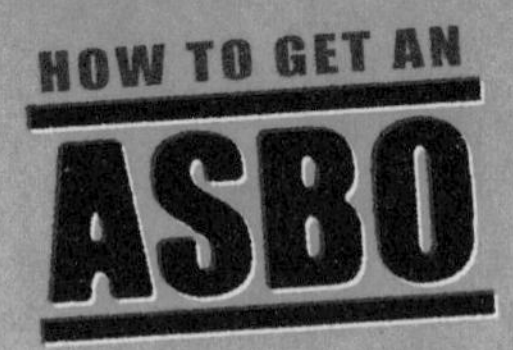

Please don't 'it me: I've got a weak 'eart innit? If I die, dat will be murder!

– Excuse me, doorman, would you refrain from hitting me. I have a weak constitution and if you do hit me you may be charged with murder if I die.

Look at me, man: I'm iced and bling bling, innit!

– I'm under the impression that a poor fake designer shirt from the market, a pair of white loafers and a chunky nine-carat kerbstone necklace makes me look like a gangster rapper.

Of course I'm eighteen, yeah? Look at me goatee!

– Surely you must be convinced that I am eighteen years old: look at the bum fluff I have grown on my chin.

Yeah, dat's right, ladies, I own ma own business and I 'ave a Beemer outside!
– I'm a part-time market stallholder at the Sunday boot fair, who lives with his mother and drives a moped.

If you play ya cards right, I'll take ya for a meal, innit?
– If you are lucky I might buy you a small donner kebab while we walk back to my mother's house.

I'll say I'm wiv dat milf, then I'll get in!
– I am going to pretend that I'm accompanying that older lady in the hope that the doorman will not question my age.

Now you know the basics of ASBO speak it's time to venture out into the real world. Good luck and remember to practise that accent.

The ASBO Family

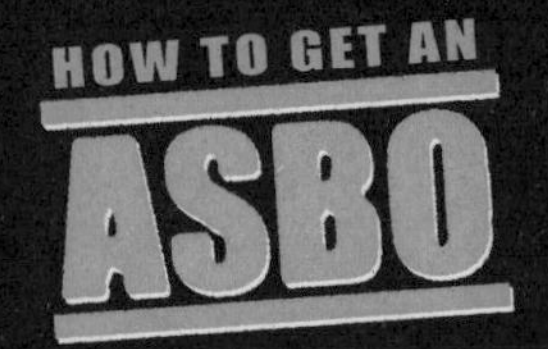

Family. Blood thicker than water. If you feel a desperate desire to obtain an ASBO, then the feeling could well be part of your inherent nature, and chances are that at least half your family members feel the same way and want one too. If you have an entire family who want to join in, so much the better. ASBOs are much more fun as a game the whole family can play, and your community will enjoy giving various labels to your troublesome clan: Mouthy, Tarty and Nutter will go well with most surnames.

But will they be a help or hindrance in your ASBO quest?

Dad – If there is one in the family then this is indeed unusual, since ASBO dads tend to be more of the wandering-star variety and will consider it a public duty to start many of their own franchises through any given town (or possibly the entire country if they are more of a adventurer). While this will mean that you may have grown up with no male role model, it will mean that, when you go to pick your ASBO crew (see 'Brothers' on page 47), you will have far more choice to cherry-pick the best of your 'bad-ass' siblings. If Dad is

'Got these knuckle dusters at the pound shop!'

about, he will usually either be completely ineffectual and spend most of his time wondering where he has gone wrong, or he will view himself as some sort of wise ASBO Gandalf and take it upon himself to impart and dispense useful advice. Rarely will this advice be on how to be a better person, but more on how to get an accurate aim when flinging Maltesers at policemen's hats at the local fair.

The unfortunate thing with this is that, like all dads, he might mean well but his advice will be about fifteen years out of date (could be less: most ASBO dads, like their female counterparts, will only be barely legally older than their sprogs). Remember, they didn't have ASBOs in their day. If you did a crime you either went to jail or got off scot-free.

Possibly because ASBO Mum has difficulty controlling her temper in public, ASBO Dad will often be called upon to appear on local news saying how his kids are being victimised by the police/council/everyone in a ten-mile exclusion zone, and they are 'high-spirited' or 'just being boys'. To make the most of their TV appearance, and so as not to cause anyone to have to rethink a stereotype, ASBO Dad should have a short haircut, be unshaven, wear a sleeveless vest-style top (in mid-November) and have various faded and therefore unrecognisable tattoos.

Mum – The matriarch of your family, and possibly to most onlookers the most obviously frightening. She might not vandalise cars or smash windows (unless of course you count her glass-shattering screeching at the kids), but she will be there all the time and will never let an argument drop. Her tenacity is to be admired, since, even when she gets her ASBO, she will never let the argument lie.

If the neighbours dare to complain to her about this, she will totally ignore them or stick them on her hate list and will go out of her way to think of things that will annoy them even more. If they complain to anyone in authority, she will treat this as a declaration of all-out war and is likely to turn around any accusations from her neighbours that she had everything done to her first.

The words 'your mum' are also great in getting any ASBO-worth scrap started. Although you might well hate your mum and agree that she is indeed 'an ugly fat tart', the very idea of someone saying this within your earshot is a perfectly legitimate reason to have a go, and you can then claim you gave them a pasting in defence of your family honour.

Sister – Depending on whether you are male or female, your sister will either be your partner in crime or the one neighbourhood slapper you have to defend. Two sisters have a long and fruitful relationship that begins with one kicking the shopkeeper's legs to make him let go of the other one's pigtails as he catches her pilfering Jelly Tots, progresses through to arguing over whose boyfriend is the harder, to appearing on *The Jeremy Kyle Show* arguing about who's the worst mother/biggest alcoholic/most prolific off-street ranter.

If you are male, your sister will be like a younger and far less useful version of your mum. Although you might hate your sister and agree with most of the things the neighbourhood says about her, you will be duty-bound to defend her. You will also possibly be required by your parents to 'look out' for your sister and, since she shares

'I'm bloody gorgeous, init!'

a set of genes with you, the chances are she will be sniffing that ASBO as surely as you are. Therefore, your duties will probably involve stopping her getting a pasting from other girls she has sneered at, helping her acquire 'smoking materials' for a reasonable price and pulling her off your mates after chugging three bottles of Lambrini on a Saturday night.

Brothers – If you're an ASBO girl your brothers are your security system. No matter what you fancy doing, you can scare people with the threat of your brothers. For the guys themselves, though, it is a proven statistic that getting an ASBO is up to 78 per cent easier if you have one brother or more.

As they knew well in the Wild West, all law bending is easier and more fun if you have your own family posse.

Ideally, you should all be like-minded (want an ASBO) but, like a team in a heist movie, you should each have a specialisation (in the business of getting an ASBO, in this case), so that you can all draw on each member's expertise. Unlike with a heist movie and more with a western, the law will work on the assumption that one of you is the ringleader, and, if they can bring down that one, all the others will fall into line. But the real truth is far more like the case of the Hydra of Greek mythology: if you cut off one head of the monster, another, nastier, drooling one grows back in its place.

'Mmm bucky!'

So there you have it, The basic structure of the ASBO family. Similar to the Addams Family, but a bit weirder and slightly more inbred-looking.

Old ASBO Wives' Tales

- **If you open an umbrella in the house you'll lose your ASBO**
- **If you pick your nose your ASBO will fall off**
- **If a black cat crosses your path you'll be banned from hanging around in bus stops**
- **If you put shoes on the table your Compensation Money won't come through**
- **If the wind changes and you're smiling, you'll lose your pram face scowl for good**
- **If you break a mirror you'll have seven years of your neighbours liking you**
- **If you hang a horseshoe over your door you'll always have a handy blunt object.**

- See a penny, pick it up all day long your friends will call you a pikey
- To predict the sex of an unborn baby dangle a wedding ring over the stomach of the mother-to-be. To predict the father go on *Jeremy Kyle*
- If you get out of bed on the wrong side... you might wake her husband up
- It is bad luck to step on a crack in the pavement, but good luck if you can prove the crack was there because the council was negligent
- A rabbit's foot will bring you luck, a cow's foot will bring you some weird looks and a human foot will bring a visit from the police
- Opals are very bad luck...especially if the previous owner has proof it's theirs.

ASBO in Love

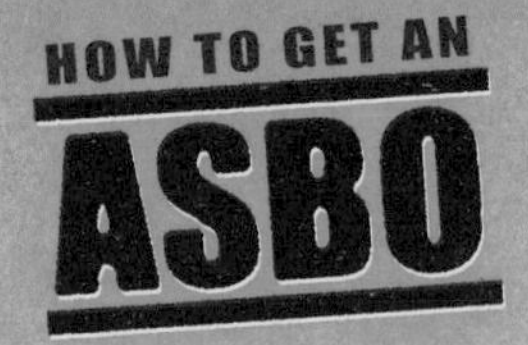

As you can see daily on any ITV morning chat show, for those who don't have a lot of real drama in their lives it can often be easier to ignite the flame of troublemaking with a lover than with a stranger. If you can find a partner who annoys you to the point of insanity, you can devote every day to making their life a total misery (with the added bonus that everyone who lives near you will get to join in as you take almost every spat into the surrounding area).

But finding love isn't always easy, and it is almost certain that you will have to kiss a lot of frogs/mingers before you find that prince/tarty bint. But this is very time-consuming,

'We just wanna be togevver!'

and, if you have to go through life rejecting all partners who just want to get on and live their lives quietly, you could end up wasting a lot of time. Therefore, we have kindly created the useful ASBO Dating Questionnaire. Simply hand this to any prospective partner you like the look of in a pub/club/

GR8LEGZ

government agency office, and you're well on your way to true ASBO love. (This questionnaire is also available in TXT Speak – love should be an equal-opportunities opportunity.)

'I love you, can I 'ave some of dat milkshake?'

Name –

Age –
Real Age –
(If you're not forced to add on at least five years for legality, or knock off ten for reasons of decency it's just not worth the bother.)

Occupation –
('Mouthy Bitch' isn't an actual occupation, but in this case it will count *for* you.)

Smoker/Non Smoker – Delete as applicable. (But if deleting 'smoker' there's not much point going any further.)

Non Drinker/Social Drinker/Drinker/Heavy Drinker/Raging Alky – Delete as applicable. (See 'Smoker' question for advice on acceptable answers.)

Past History Section
Please list the names of all previous partners from the last five years (an extra sheet can be added if needed). Try to include their relationship to you and any outstanding injunctions you have on each other. Do not add one-night stands to this list – simply round them up and settle on an estimated figure.

Please list the names of all children you have whom you are aware of. Make mention if they live with you, or if you are still allowed within 100 yards of their mother/father. If names cannot be remembered, rough ages will be acceptable. (Those over the age of 12 need not be added unless you will expect the potential applicant to accompany you to the court hearings/youth offender centre visits.)

Interests Section

Favourite Song –

(Please state the volume at which you would enjoying listening to this and how many times in a row you would choose to hear it.)

Favourite TV Show –

(Do you like this show so much that, if the television was turned over while it was on, you might have the potential to throw the set out of the window?)

Favourite Meal –

(Any item available at the chip shop will count as a meal.)

Favourite Sport –

(You are not allowed to count baseball even though you own a bat.)

Morality section

If I cheated on you, or you thought I might be thinking of it, what would you do? (Please add the names of friends that could be phoned in order to bail you out, preferred casualty units and 24-hour free solicitor.)

I am arrested for a minor and petty crime. Please list the kinds of names you would shout at the arresting officer, and describe the kind of unsuitable outfit you would wear if you had to then visit me on remand.

Hopes and Aspirations section

Would you like to have more children? (The correct answer is yes. Doesn't matter how many you already have. Nothing says true ASBO love like a baby together.)

Where do you see yourself in five years' time? (If you cannot think that far ahead, simply write 'dunno')

Wedding Etiquette

	DON'T	DO
If the occasion requires you to be suited and booted...	Hire a suit from your local gentleman's outfitters.	Wear your favourite shellsuit and prison white trainers.
The groom has requested a quiet stag night...	Take him out for a few drinks with friends and reminisce about good times, making sure he's back in his own bed by midnight.	Get him blind drunk and take him on a magical mystery tour that leaves him stark naked, his bollocks painted blue, tied to a lampost on the Scottish border.
As the best man, you have to write a speech...	Mention what a fabulous chap he is and how he'll make a great husband.	Mention that fling with his ex's mother, 'that night in Hamburg' and all his other conquests, two of whom happen to be bridesmaids!
As the best man, it's your duty to bring the rings...	Check that you have them just before you leave for the church, so there are no upsets.	Pawn the rings for cash. Just before the ceremony, tell the groom you've forgotten them and one of your faux sovereign rings will do!

One of the bridesmaids starts to flirt with you…	Compliment her on how beautiful she looks in that dress but explain that you are already married.	Suggest you both find a secluded area for a 'quickie'.
When the bride and groom cut the cake…	Take some of your own photographs to capture the happy moment.	Say loudly 'I don't like fruit cake and that looks nothing like them on the top… have you got any doughnuts?'
At the reception buffet…	Help yourself to a light meal to soak up some of that alcohol you've consumed.	Gorge yourself as if you haven't eaten for a week and upon seeing some smoked salmon, loudly say 'This fish is minging, have you got any chicken nuggets?'
As the bride and groom leave for their honeymoon…	Wish them all the best for the future and hope they have a great honeymoon.	Say to another guest, 'I've been to that resort, it's crap! I'll give it six months!'

ASBO Education

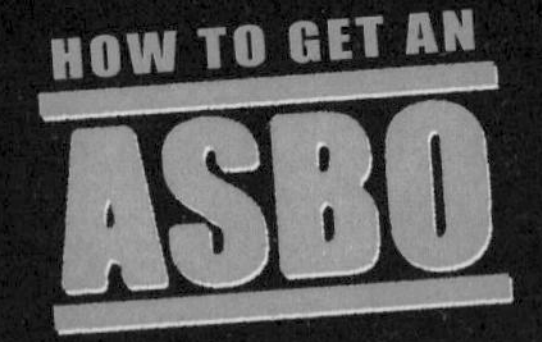

If you happen to be below the age of 16, your ASBO quest may be hindered somewhat, in that you will be expected to devote at least six hours per day not to your potential ASBO, but to the place they call 'school'. Of course if you're creative enough you will find that this is not as bad as it might sound and that you can use the facilities as a great first step up on the ASBO ladder. Good beginnings are always important, and it's school that will give you your first taste of institutional correction that you're hoping will last you a lifetime.

An early start

If it's in your blood, your behaviour pattern will have already been set by the time you begin primary school. There are many ways in which you can get yourself 'my first ASBO' from your teachers, and now is the time for experimenting with what suits you best. You could pick some of your fellow classmates and randomly whack them with paintbrushes every time you go near them until you get removed to your own corner of the classroom. But don't let this stop you: you can just continue chucking stickle bricks at them from a distance (also helping you develop your missile-throwing skills for the future).

Eventually, you will get sent to the office of the head, when you will employ your first use of another life skill: looking innocent. This will work better for you as an angelic-looking five-year-old than when you are a twenty-year-old, unshaven Grant Mitchell lookalike, but it will make those in authority question how someone so cute/dim-looking could do such terrible things, and it must all be a terrible misunderstanding.

At this point (don't worry – they will probably disown you later), you'll have your parents to come in and plead your case for you. Whereas posh or middle-class parents might try to repress family problems or deny they exist, your parents should be of the type who ensure that your terrible home life is a get-out-of-jail-free card for anything dreadful you are doing and you should be applauded for being as normal as you are against such great hardships. You will then be placed back in a regular classroom environment and then you can really get creative.

The middle years

This is the time frame for pupils that all schoolteachers dread: old enough to know how to work the system but still a little too young to bunk off into shopping centres. All your time can be devoted to this new womb of ASBO testing.

After the 'blame-free' culture of the early years of school, the middle years will introduce you for the first time to punishment.

Pink Floyd might have warned of 'dark sarcasm in the classroom', but, if a teacher tries anything so distressing on you, you can claim this led to feelings of low self-esteem, forcing you to glue the speccy kid to his lunchbox in order to regain feelings of self-worth. Academia, you will no doubt have noted by now, will serve you no practical purpose in achieving an ASBO.

'We're on a school trip, honest!'

History – **It's all happened already.**

Geography – **You're not lost.**

Maths – **You've either got money or not. It's not worth counting it.**

French – **They speak English on the ferry so what's the point? You won't be getting off after you've filled the car with booze and fags.**

Yes, your school years are the best of your life. Just remember: if your ASBO mission is a success and leads to greater things, you'll be glad of the time you spent early on honing those skills.

MFINK

School Etiquette

	DON'T	DO
It's time for the morning school run…	Leave in plenty of time, driving as carefully and considerately as you normally do.	Leave at the last minute, driving in such an aggressive and inconsiderate manner you'd put a white van man to shame.
Your little darling is picked to be one of the sheep in the nativity play…	Think it is great that your child is in the play and look forward to the performance.	Find the drama/music teacher, explain that your child is going to be a professional actor and if they aren't given the lead role, you'll have them sacked.
At the performance of the school play…	Wait nervously for your child's scene and become overwhelmed with emotion when the scene starts.	Mercilessly mock other children's performances in between making shouty calls on your mobile phone.

Your child has their mobile phone stolen at school, allegedly by another pupil.	Go to the school office and explain the situation to the schools representative in a calm and reasoned fashion.	March into the school and as soon as you find the nearest teacher or receptionist scream at the top of your lungs that you are going to sue the child's teachers, all the pupils in their class and the local education authority before your child finally confesses that they've in fact sold the phone and concocted this alleged theft.
Your 12-year-old child is caught smoking at school and has their cigarettes confiscated by a teacher…	Ensure the school that the child will be further punished when they get home and ask the school to destroy the cigarettes.	Ask the school for the cigarettes back as you 'paid good money for them' and dish out a cigarette to your child as soon as you leave school property.

ASBO Fairy Tales

The ASBO Duckling

❄ ❄ ❄ ❄ ❄

Once upon a time in a lovely farm in the country there lived Mummy Duck and Daddy Duck. One day, Mummy Duck and Daddy Duck were blessed with six wonderful eggs. When the eggs hatched, five of the ducklings were just perfect little babies who liked to swim and catch fish and follow Mummy Duck all around the pond; but the sixth little duckling looked a bit manky and had most of his feathers missing. He didn't quite quack like all the others, couldn't swim and seemed to cause trouble and annoyance wherever he went.

His brothers and sisters would go out of their way not to play with him and pretend they did not see him or did not know him. This made Mummy and Daddy Duck very sad.

The farmer became very distressed at this and was worried this duckling might have some kind of bird flu, and so he chucked out the weird-looking duckling so that he wouldn't contaminate the egg production of the other ducks.

The poor ugly duckling was very sad (although

the rest of his family were secretly rather pleased) and wandered up and down hiding away from other birds. Then one day he came to a large town – indeed, a city. He was very frightened at all the noise of this city. Then things went from bad to worse when he found himself being pecked at by a gang of London pigeons.

'Don't you come raaahnd 'ere and nick our bread,' they squawked.

'What the bleedin' 'ell are you on about?' the ASBO duckling sniffed back. 'I'm a duckling. I'm looking for a pond to live in quietly because no one loves me.'

'Don't give me that load of old fanny,' said the London pigeons. 'You're nothing special raaahnd here. There's loads of us pigeons.' And they flew off (because he was a bit bigger than them and still quite mangy-looking).

'A pigeon?' said the duckling. 'Surely not.' But, sure enough, he found a statue and fountain and there through the algae and litter he saw the reflection of a very tough-looking pigeon!

'Hooray!' said the ASBO duckling. 'I'm a pigeon!

I can spend the rest of my life happily spreading fleas and disease and shitting on people! That'll show the bastardly world! Now, where are those other pigeons? It's pecking payback time!'

And so the ASBO duckling lived happily ever after, making life just that little bit more shitty for all around him.

Chavarella

❄ ❄ ❄ ❄ ❄

Once upon a time there was a beautiful young girl (OK, not that beautiful, but she did have nice hair and all her own teeth) who was stupid enough to do all the cleaning in the house for her stepmother and her two minging stepsisters. One day she learned that Dazza, the cutest boy who lived in the flats, was having an all-nighter and had invited all the girls who lived around there, so long as they brought some cheap vodka and wore short skirts.

Chavarella's sisters (who had far worse hair and not so many of their own teeth) told Chavarella she was not going to go and if they saw her there they would kick her squarely into next week and tell Dazza she was 'a downstairs wart hostel'. So, sadly, Chavarella resigned herself to the fact that she was going to have to stay home and watch Footballers' Wives instead.

As she sat on her sofa crying, there was a knock on the door and Tarty Tracy from downstairs appeared. She felt very sorry for Chavarella and revealed that she had promised Chavarella's dad, before he got banged up, that she would look out for his 'little princess'. (She had promised this one night in the back of his car but didn't feel the need to mention this part of the story, although everyone, including Chavarella, pretty much knew this anyway.) With the aid of a bottle of Born Blonde superstrength and industrial amounts of slap, Chavarella was transformed! And she did indeed go to the all-nighter, where she danced the 'mattress mambo' all night with Dazza.

At midnight she remembered she'd left the telly on and rushed off home before her stepmother ran out of booze and started walking the streets looking for either more booze or one of her daughters.

The next day, through his hangover, Dazza remembered that one of the girls had been slightly more fragrant than the others, and resolved that if ever he settled down it would be with someone his mates would say 'Phwor!' about, rather than 'Ugh!' But how would he ever find this fragrant young lady?

As luck would have it, nine months later on a daytime talk show (he had been forced to go on by half the neighbourhood slappers), he had the answer. He realised all he had to do was sniff all the girls waiting for the results of the paternity tests and the one who didn't stink of old sweat, fags and cheap perfume was the one!

As the girls came one by one to scream in his face about maintenance and slap him, he breathed in their odour, and at last was reunited with Chavarella, whom he resolved to have move in with him at once. Yes, he had to admit that some of the babies were his, but it was all worth it in the end.

And as for Chavarella? Well, even though her baby's daddy was also her niece and nephew's daddy, she lived happily ever after.

The Three Little ASBO Pigs

❄ ❄ ❄ ❄ ❄

Once upon a time there were three little pigs who for no reason we know the answer to did not live on a farm but instead with their mother. One day Mother Pig (who was a bit of a gin fiend on the quiet) read how much money she could make if she chucked out her brood and rented their rooms to Albanian students. So without delay she told them it was 'time to make your way in the world' and sent them packing (probably with one of those stupid handkerchief-on-a-stick luggage combos they seem so fond of in these kinds of tale).

Before the little pigs could say 'no fixed abode' they got themselves off to the local housing authority quick-smart and were promptly informed that, since they had no dependants, mental-health problems or addictions that were causing them to self-harm, they had no entitlement to government-sponsored housing. The man behind the bulletproof glass with the bolted-down chair suggested that, if they came back within six months and brought a note from any therapist, he could maybe get them on a 'self-build' help scheme – but he couldn't promise anything.

This gave the pigs a great idea. They used to be quite good with Lego and shit, so they would build their own homes! Sadly for the little pigs, they did not realise they were being watched by Bad Wolfie Daddy, the local pimp who ran a lucrative trade in selling young piggies to a 'specialist market'. He hung around all the places where he knew desperate young piggies could be found and procured, and he followed them.

Again, for no good reason, they all seemed to

think it was a good idea to build separate houses, and the first little pig went off to the back of Tesco and fashioned himself a house from boxes. Soon Wolfie came a-calling and within seconds the first little pig found himself being taken on a lovely visit to Porky Lumps Meat Emporium.

The second little pig ended up down the canal with the winos and hid himself under a discarded fire door and was easy pickings when Wolfie came by and offered to buy him a double cheeseburger with extra gherkin.

The third (and not as congenitally stupid as his brothers) little piggy was far more sensible. He managed to find himself a place in a fairly decent squat in a block of derelict flats, as he realised his building skills were really not up to scratch. Although he was tempted when Wolfie came by offering to introduce him to kind 'pork-loving gentlemen', he remained steadfast and Wolfie soon gave up when he realised the lifts never worked and there were easier pickings than a pig who lived at the top of eighteen flights of stairs.

The third little piggy mourned his brothers, sued his mother for negligence and lived happily ever after.

ASBO Goldilocks and the Three Bears

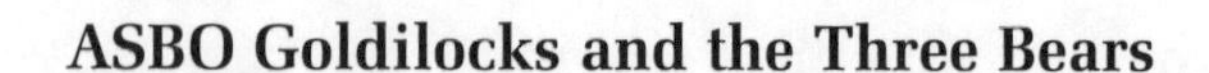

Once upon a time there was a law-abiding family of bears. Although they struggled with a world that was biased towards humans, they got on remarkably well and did lots of things together as a family unit. One Sunday, Mummy Bear made some porridge for breakfast. Of course, we all know that bears are actually carnivores (with an occasional liking for honey), and so we can only assume that they were living on the poverty line and were forced to eat cheap grains.

Anyway, as they sat down to eat it, Daddy Bear and Baby Bear remarked how hot it was, and, to her great credit, Mummy Bear did not tell them where they could stuff it and instead suggested it would be a good idea to go out for a walk while it cooled down. (Bears are not known for their skills of rationality in working out how long food takes to cool.)

Of course, because the three bears lived on a rather rough estate, their going outside at such an early time was noted by every lawbreaker living within a mile radius. Sadly for the bears, Goldilocks decided to pay them a visit. Goldilocks (or Blondie Light Fingers, as she was sometimes known) didn't find their house as difficult to get into as some of her other house-breaking adventures (bears are also not good at laying man traps or even putting in security cameras), and got right in through the open bathroom window. This

was quite easy, because Goldie was fairly undernourished and small. This also meant she was usually hungry. Hungry enough to try to eat the bears' poverty porridge.

Goldilocks was used to a diet of things that went with chips and so found the porridge quite disgusting and spat Daddy Bear's bowlful up the walls, dumped Mummy Bear's on the floor and stuffed Baby Bear's in a cushion cover.

Looking round the house, Goldilocks was angered to find the bears had nothing good to steal

and so smashed their living room furniture, as it was 'too cheap and crap'. After all this activity she got rather worn out and decided to have a poke round the bedrooms, either to find some more booty or to ring her gang on her mobile (peasant bears didn't even have a landline!) to get them to come round and help her trash the place further. Goldie had been out on the razz all night and thought she might take a nap. The stupid bears had probably gone to Bear Church or something. But, as we all know, they hadn't. After about ten minutes, Mummy bear realised the porridge would almost have turned into wallpaper paste by now and, if they didn't return, it would be uneatable, and they couldn't afford the food wastage (or dentists' bills if it gummed Baby Bear's teeth together), so they returned home.

The bears were most upset when they saw what had been done to their home. But, unfortunately for Goldilocks (but very fortunately for the rest of the estate), that sadness soon turned to anger as they spotted her sprawled across one of the beds, snoring. The bears quickly remembered that they were carnivores and some things tasted a lot better than porridge.

ASBO
Songs

It's never too young to start going for that ASBO, and even tiny tots can be encouraged from the earliest of ages just by putting the ideas as part of their everyday lives into their nursery rhymes and fairy tales ...

Monday's ASBO is spotty of face.
Tuesday's ASBO is sprayed with mace.
Wednesday's ASBO buys some blow.
Thursday's ASBO is a bit slow.
Friday's ASBO is smelly and minging.
Saturday's ASBO nicks cars for a living.
But the ASBO dished out on the Sabbath day
Is the one that will have your purse away.

Georgie Porgie pudding and pie
Knocked up a bird and told a lie;
When his wife discovered this play,
Georgie's missus was done for affray.

Oh, do you know the ASBO man –
The ASBO man, the ASBO man?
Yes, I know the ASBO man –
He's always up in court.

Humpty ASBO leant on a wall,
Smokin' fags and kickin' a ball;
All the school's teachers and all of the rozzers
Couldn't make Humpty say he was bovvered.

Baa, baa ASBO dog, listen to you bark –
Big teeth, big teeth, sharper than a shark
Howls at its master, bites at its dame
Growls at the little boy who lives down the lane.

The grand old Duke of Chav,
He had ten thousand kids;
He marched them off to stay at his mum's –
And then he left them there.

This little townie hung out at market;
This little townie played Playstation at home;
This little townie had Maccie D's;
This little townie got stoned;
And this little townie played drum and bass
In his car – all the way home.

Wouldn't It Be Nice to Get on with Your Neighbours?

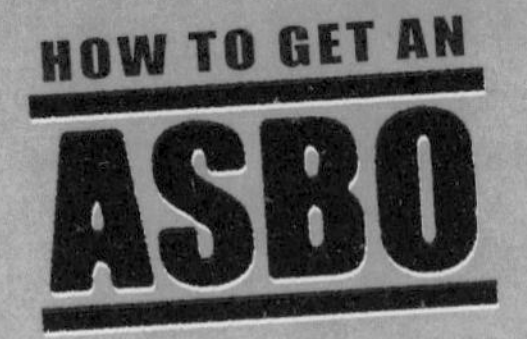

It doesn't matter if you have just flown the nest or been evicted from your previous abode, there are certain things you have to do when you move to a new house. The first is to secure your new dwelling with a couple of (hopefully breeding) guard dogs. Forget traditional guard-dog breeds such as Rottweilers and Dobermans – they'll be prohibitively expensive and possibly trainable.

The ideal place to pick up a couple of faithful friends is the local rescue centre. What you should be looking for are bull terrier breeds that have been abused and abandoned by another ASBO-seeker. If you are lucky you might come across the ASBO warrior's dog breed Nirvana, the American pit-bull cross. Not only will this dog be as mad as a lorry with aggression, but will impress the hell out of your buddies that you have an animal that skirts the boundaries of the Dangerous Dogs Act.

Once you have your pair of ASBO dogs, you must familiarise them with their new environment: your back garden, or, as it's soon to be known, the dogs' toilet. You may notice that the fence surrounding your back garden has many holes and your faithful friends are likely to escape. However, it is essential that you do not buy anything

'What's wrong with 'aving a 30ft garden gnome?'

either to fix your fence or chain up your canine soldiers. This money needs to be spent on your stadium speaker system and cellar of continental lager.

Don't bother with an expensive kennel: an internal door taken from your place and leaned up against the outside of your house makes a perfect home for two hardy dogs, whatever the weather. You will find that your pampered pooches will thank you for their new home by howling every night in appreciation!

Once your back garden has been turned over to a dog toilet, naturally your focus will turn to your front garden

'Turn the music daahn? You can f**k off!'

and the myriad possibilities it holds. Perhaps an alpine shrubbery or maybe a Japanese water garden? However, after another hard day cheesing the neighbourhood off, you will no doubt decide to put your feet up in front of the TV and let your front garden develop organically. Naturally, after you've been six months in your new home, your front garden will have developed its own theme of 'urban decay'.

If you're not a music lover but are good with your hands, DIY and gardening might be the key to getting that ASBO. One of the easiest projects you could try is the cultivation of the famous leylandii tree. All you need to do is plonk a few saplings at the bottom of your back garden and watch them grow – literally. Within a couple of years, they will have grown so tall that they'll block out the sun from your neighbour's house, frightening the entire community into thinking there might be a Triffid invasion. Naturally, many a garden-fence argument will ensue, with plenty of opportunity to get featured on such TV shows as *Next-Door Nuisance from Planet Hell.*

Community. It's a word that you might not be able to spell but don't let anyone suggest you don't know the real meaning behind it.

TOP 10

ASBO Illnesses & Ailments

We all know that people who are unwell can't help it but sometimes the illnesses and ailments they have are just very annoying to those around them. Antisocial in fact.

1. **Colds and Flu** – The sufferer just has to pass it round so everyone can be as miserable as they are.

2. **Coughs** – There's only so much sympathy you can have for someone with a cough before they really start to annoy you. They usually decide a good spluttering fit is best placed at the most quiet or emotional point in a film or play.

3. **Acne** – If someone has bad enough acne, you do believe they might erupt all over you or your dinner.

4 **Halitosis** – An ailment so antisocial you won't be able to talk to people without them fleeing.

5 **Smelly Feet** – Upon entering anyone's house they will think you have trod in something nasty. Until they realise your feet are the nasty.

6 **Dandruff** – It is nice to share, but that doesn't include bits of scalp.

7 **Athlete's Foot** – See Dandruff...but with bare feet.

8 **Head Lice** – The pet of choice for many children.

9 **Indigestion** – Knowledge is power, but not many people want to be able to tell what you had for dinner just by sniffing.

10 **Wind** – See Indigestion. Crossed with bad feet and halitosis the person afflicted can be registered as a human chemical weapon.

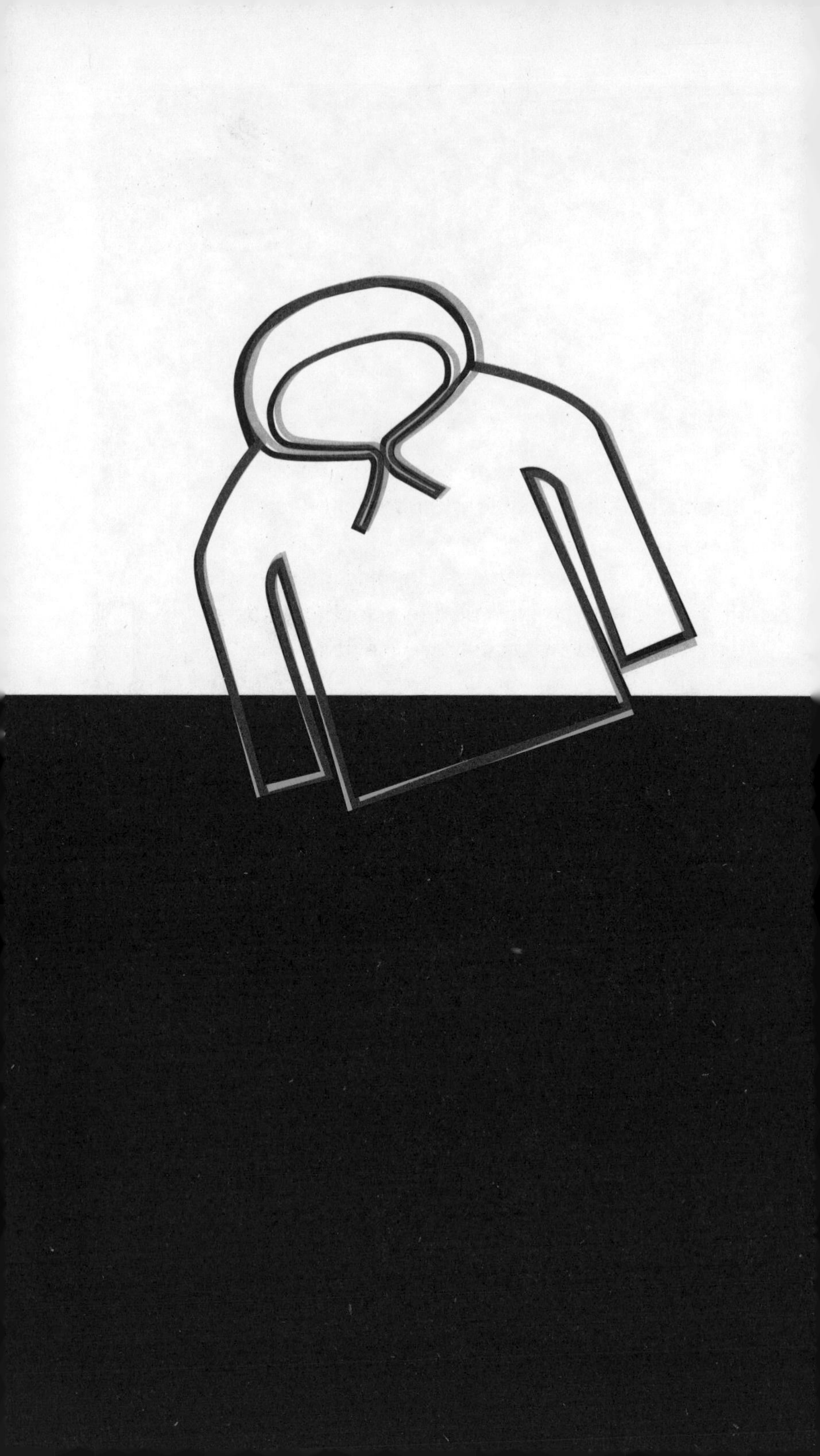

ASBO
Attitude

Half of the battle in getting anything is looking as if you belong. If you want to get your ASBO you have to have the right attitude, and if you can look as if you have it then you're halfway there. You will not get an ASBO for being reasonable and open to other opinions. So here, just to clear up any potential confusion, we have some handy points to developing your ASBO attitude.

Attitude Checklist

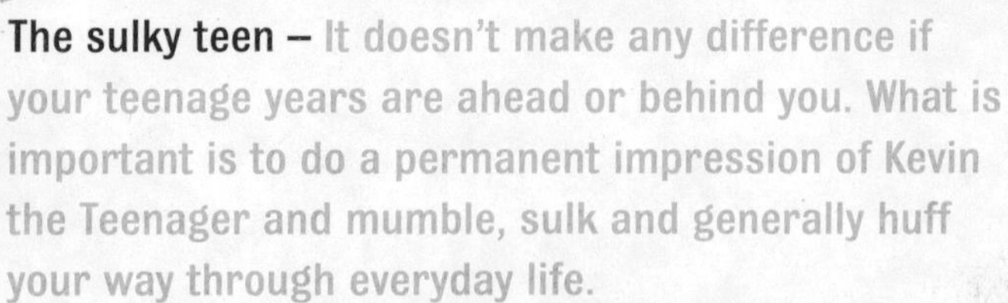

The sulky teen – It doesn't make any difference if your teenage years are ahead or behind you. What is important is to do a permanent impression of Kevin the Teenager and mumble, sulk and generally huff your way through everyday life. ✓

The lack of basic manners – 'Please' and 'thank you'? For losers only. Why should you bother to defer to people you're obviously way better than? ✓

Cont...

The scowl – It might make you look brooding and moody, and most probably it makes you look a bit of a tit, but in any case you must never smile. Ever. That might cause people to think you're friendly or approachable, and that is not something you want when you're trying to get people to fear you.

Failure to make eye contact – They say you can't look someone in the eye and tell them a lie. So in that case don't ever look them in the eye. This might annoy people and cause them great frustration as they feel they can't ever really get to know or like you. ASBO result!

The stare – In direct contrast to not making eye contact, the quickest way to pick a fight with a fellow ASBO-seeker is to 'look at them a bit funny'. They will imagine any number of things that you are thinking about them and will use this as an excuse to begin rucking (as if they actually need one).

Cont...

Rejection of consonants – Your speech pattern should be virtually incomprehensible to anyone other than fellow ASBO-seekers and should sound like a high-pitched whine of someone repeating all the vowels in a random order. If you use this, combined with the failure to make eye contact, 98 per cent of the rest of the population will have no idea what you are trying to say and this will be a bonus when your solicitor or social worker translates for you.

The walk – As well as talking the talk you will need to walk the walk, and this can best be described as a kind of sub-chimpanzee swing in which you hunch over a little, keep your legs far apart and swing one arm menacingly. Special mention should be given to remembering to give your crotch area a little squeeze or tickle every five minutes or so.

Incredulousness – After you've spent all this time making everyone think you're a 'bad lot', you have to be shocked beyond belief when they agree that you are. Then you can complain about harassment and being picked on. It won't wash with anyone but your mum, but you have to give it a go.

Still not sure whether you're doing it right? Well, here are some people who have got it off to perfection or simply don't have a clue.

People with the right attitude

The local tramp

People with the wrong attitude

Ant and Dec
Ronan Keating
Phillip Schofield
James Blunt

Innocent ASBOs

You may not think you're doing anything wrong and not even trying to get an ASBO but if ASBO wants you, you can get one for doing almost anything. Here's some we think might be on the cards for some well-known characters…

Yogi Bear and Boo Boo
Stealing picnic baskets

Woody Woodpecker
Excessive pecking and noise-making

Mr Spoon from *Button Moon*
Revving his Baked Bean Can rocket at unsociable hours

Top Cat
Disrespect to the police, living in unsanitary dustbins, having a coin on a string ....the list is endless!

Big Bird from *Sesame Street*
Keeping an exotic pet (Mr Snuffleupagus) in cramped conditions with no licence

Tom and Jerry

A sustained campaign of domestic violence

Captain Caveman

Brandishing a large bat and shouting at passers-by

Bert from *Mary Poppins*

Drawing on pavements with no arts council licence

Huckleberry Finn

Trout-poaching and failing to attend school

Wil-E-Coyote

Feeding and attempting to eat wildfowl in public

The Magic Roundabout

A plethora of ASBOs just waiting to happen.
An unlicensed fairground attraction, an unmuzzled dog and a loose cow in clothing. Not even to mention Zebedes' dangerous-looking spring

Spit the Dog

Unhygienic habits. Also very unkempt and dirty-looking.
Might well have a flea infestation

The Gang from *Scooby Doo*

Breaking into 'haunted' amusment parks and helping themselves to (bizarrely) fully stocked refrigerators, to make foot-high sandwiches

The Smurfs

Going round without shirts all the time

Hong Kong Phooey

Unlawful use of martial arts. Since he is a dog he probably doesn't have a driving licence either

Mr Benn

Wasting the time of shopkeepers when he never has any intention of making a purchase

Animal from *The Muppets*

Drumming and unnecessary noise-making. Harassment of women

Rod, Jane and Freddy from *Rainbow*

General crimes against music and fashion

Roobarb and Custard

Sitting on fences and hurling abuse at each other

Secret Squirrel

Peeping Tom

The Tracy Family From *Thunderbirds*

Keeping military-style vehicles and equipment in a residential area

Dick Dastardly

Speeding, trying to entrap pigeons and sarcasm towards pet dog

TOP 10 *Weirdo ASBOS*

Behaving badly will probably guarantee you getting an ASBO, but just to make it fair on everyone, occasionally the ASBO world will throw up a real surprise...

*(All names and situations have been changed as they are in fact, made up)

1. Mrs Janet Tableflute was banned from thinking about Luciano Pavarotti outside of her home for the next three years, after she thought about him while walking her dog and forgot to use her Poopy Scoopy, causing an unfortunate dog muck/shoe incident to a local councillor.

2. Sharon Weberckering (23) of West Barlow was prohibited from using hair-styling products during

daytime hours. Police were concerned that the height and density of her styled bonce may constitute a public menace.

3 Mr Tony Needleshoff of Spezex-New Town has been banned from all auto-repair centres in his county for the next five years after an incident at his local Kwik Fit in which he accused all the fitters of being members of the LNF (Liberation of Norway Foundation) and instead of fitting a new exhaust and back tyre, they had in fact fitted a tracking device and a poison dart blower. Mr Needleshoff's care worker argued that he would now have to visit overpriced garages for his auto repairs, but this plea held no sway with the judge and the ASBO stands.

4 Michael Careterficking (12) was issued with an ASBO for misuse of Tippex and banned from the purchase or use of liquid paper products for the remainder of his school career. Teachers said that one exam paper he handed in was almost 2 inches thick and he still didn't manage to answer the correct questions.

5 Wexford Leafgrass was issued with an ASBO that stated he must wash his hair at least once a week or face a custodial sentence. The courts were told that Mr Leafgrass's hair was operating as an unregistered flea circus and it was only the fact that he wasn't charging an entrance fee that saved him from having to pay tax on his head.

6 Sarah Barfseed faces a prison term if she eats Italian food outside of her home. The combination of garlic, onions and Parmesan cheese on her digestive system and sweat glands made her a bio-hazard to her local community, the courts were told. Her plea that she could not help it did not go unheeded and she may be able to get round her ASBO if she issues all her neighbours with a written warning before she next decides to have lasagne and garlic bread.

7 Dave Mackerding's ASBO says he has to keep track of what jokes or 'amusing' anecdotes he has told friends and workmates. Under the terms of his ASBO if he tells the same joke to the same person more than three times, they can report him to police and he may face a custodial sentence.

8 Although the most accurate player on his local darts team, not everyone appreciates Jack Widgetley's aim. His ASBO was given to him after he spent up to four years flicking bogies out of his bedroom window at the street lamps. Neighbours complained that after a particularly nasty bout of bronchitis Mr Widgetley suffered last year, the street spent almost three weeks in darkness. Under the terms of his ASBO Mr Widgetley must produce his soiled hankerchiefs at the local police station once a week.

⑨ Jilly Doggon (73) of South Deebert-on-Sea has been prohibited from talking about any book, film or television programme she has ever seen. Friends and neighbours mounted a petition and action was taken against Miss Doggon for crimes against people's sanity. One friend of hers complained that over the past 3 years she had told her the endings of the films *The Sixth Sense*, *The Crying Game* and *Finding Nemo* as well as every episode of *EastEnders* and *Miss Marple* every broadcast. If Miss Doggon breaks the condition of this ASBO, police have said she will NOT face prison due to her age, but are looking at the possibilities of fitting her with a zip.

⑩ Three siblings have fought successfully to have their parents issued with an ASBO before the birth of their new brother or sister. Foobry Jelly, Swizzle Moonbeam and Sticksy Licky-Splix Jackson all agree that the local authorities, or indeed any responsible adult, should be allowed to provide names for any of their future siblings after they (and the judge) agreed that their parents were guilty of behaving in an antisocial fashion by naming them 'as if they should be situated on the pick and mix counter'. Under the terms of the ASBO the unborn child has to be named something that does not cause a fit of the giggles in at least six independent case studies.

Comm

ASBO
unications

Communication is what separates man from animal. From the time when mankind started telling stories on cave walls with mud, through to communication via tom-tom drums and smoke signals to the invention of video mobiles, we have adapted our forms of communication to what suits us as people and a society. If you're the ASBO kind, chances are that your preferred form of communication will be the txt msg. But there are times you will want to communicate with a wider audience. Or perhaps you just can't afford any more credit.

GR8

TXT messaging

ASS

A Gr8 & cheap way of tlkn 2 yr m8s. Or, in actual English, a form of communicating with your friends that doesn't require nuance of language, intonation or any social skills whatsoever. As the previous abbreviation examples show, you don't even really need much of a grasp of English.

The important thing to remember is that you must keep any message below 160 characters, because, if you go even one over, you might have to pay for a second message, which

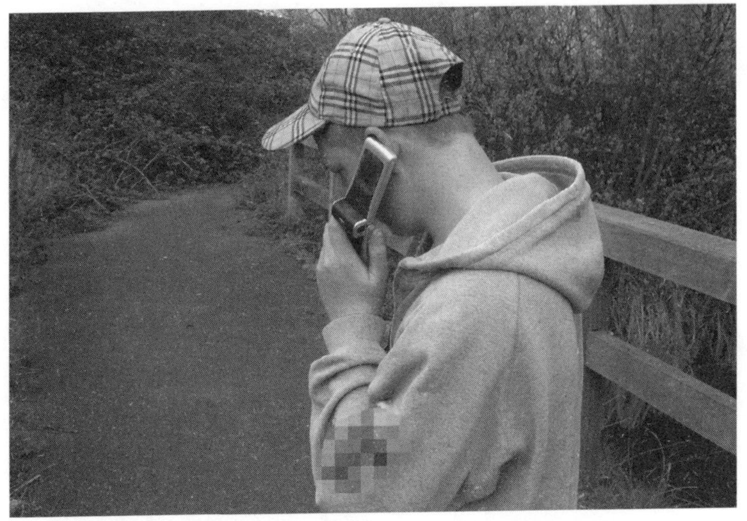

'The Phone? Yeah I just nicked it, bruv!'

could cost as much as twelve whole pence and could severely hamper your financial status for the next week. (On the other hand, though, it is perfectly acceptable to send a stream of messages such as 'no', 'yes', 'maybe' or 'fuck off', which will cost the same amount as a 160-character essay. You can't have rollover characters, sadly.)

So, since every character counts, you have to learn such stunning abbreviations as 'goin'' instead of 'going', which will save you one whole letter. Of course, it isn't so much about the saved letter as what it will say about you. You're not the kind of person to fit in with grammatical rules. Why should you spell words the same as the rest of the English-speaking world, eh?

Another positive benefit of using your mobile to send txts is that it's antisocial. As you will no doubt know already, one of the most annoying things you can do is conduct a very loud conversation on your mobile. But second only to this is sending a barrage of text messages. This is modern technology's answer to the sneaky whisper and can be used to annoy in a variety of ways.

Texting while you are in company is perhaps one of the quickest ways of earning the status of antisocial behaviour. Result.

Yes, communication is really where it's at. After all, why else are you going for that ASBO if not to let people know you're alive? With the right forms of communication they can't very well miss the fact, can they?

ASBO Style

ASBO is indeed a badge of honour, but what are you going to pin it to? What you wear says as much about you as what you do. From the teachers to the magistrates, if your clothes don't say it all within seconds of their clapping eyes on you, you're just not doing it right. So here is our guide to what to wear…ASBO Style.

Hoodie: Totally essential. So much so that very often the young ASBO-quester can be referred to as a 'hoodie'. Truly, this is a case of becoming what you wear or vice versa. But there really is far more to the humble hoody than that. Hoods on garments may have been invented to keep the wearer dry, but they also have the useful function of keeping the user's identity secret from security guards and CCTV cameras. Also since everyone wears one, your duty solicitor will be able to argue much more effectively that the hooded goblin filmed peeling the bark from trees and throttling

'I'm gonna wear dis to Bluewater!'

squirrels was not, in fact, his client but just another goblin in a remarkably similar hooded top, and the fact that his client was found covered in splinters and squirrel poo is pure coincidence.

'They're comfy yet classy, innit!'

Jogging bottoms: Comfort and practicality. Real trousers usually will involve zips and buttons and these things will take time and talent to master that could better be spent on your real interests. But the real benefit to these trousers isn't the comfy elasticated waistband but the watertight elasticated leg cuffs. If you go shopping and you run out of pocket space, these will serve as a veritable Santa's stocking for goodies and surely no one will ever notice that your legs look rather deformed and lumpy. Other useful benefits are having ready-made bicycle clips, and, even better, if you have a nervous disposition and your body tends to lose control if afraid, they should contain anything that might happen to run down your leg, and save your blushes.

'Gonna look well smart in me fake Burberry!'

Socks: No, not the type that your granny knits for Christmas but the tight elasticated kind that you can pull over your jogging bottoms in case they should ever let you down. There's no way anything is slipping down your legs with such a backed-up security system, is there? Who cares about getting your blood to circulate to your feet? If they get too tight you can always have them surgically removed in casualty.

Huge baggy jeans: Baggy jeans are a wonderful sartorial advance for those not wishing to conceal items or run very fast.

Trainers: These used to be known as running shoes, but, believe us, if you do this ASBO style, you won't be running any time soon in these. For a start, you have to look at the fastening system of laces and then remove them, or loosen them so much that they might as well not be there anyway. But the amount of space this will give you to tuck the jogging bottoms into will be more than worth any tripping over you will do. They also have to be white, white, white, and forget about tennis whitener: if you can't afford to buy a new pair once a week you're just faking it, anyway.

Baseball cap: The clever ASBO-seeker has to be on the ball at all times and knows he can never fully rely on any one clothing item to do the job, so he doesn't put all his faith in his hoody. Squeezed under the hood that is designed for only one size of head, the peak of the baseball cap can have the effect of making you look like a duck–human hybrid. No matter.

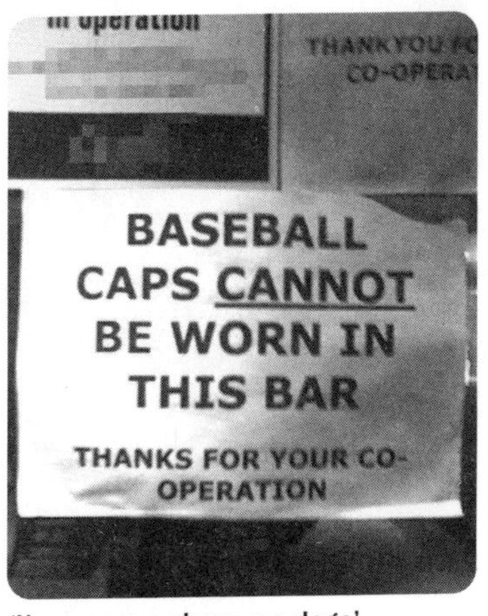

'No caps, no chavs, no dogs'

'This trackie cost me a fortune down the market!'

Branded sportswear: All of the items you will need to wear can of course be purchased anywhere. But, if you are thinking you could get your hoodie or jogging bottoms from any old store, you might as well tie the noose of ASBO social

suicide right now. Every item you wear has to be branded sports wear of the highest quality that a Far East sweatshop will allow. Please don't think that you need to have all the same sponsored brand, either: when it comes to labels, you don't have to have any loyalty, and the mix-and-match option is to be favoured, because it will get you in with any crowd. It doesn't matter that the nearest you'll ever get to the Olympics is flying over Athens on your way to Faliraki. The idea is that you look as if you're at your physical peak (as you smoke a fag and pull from the lager bottle) and could take on all-comers. Or, if not, then at the very least run away from them if need be.

Fake designer accessories: All the sportswear, however, can get a bit tiresome and you might feel the need to jazz it up to show you have many facets. How better, then, to show off some of your 'wealth' and class than by wearing your

tracksuit with a Burberry scarf or some Gucci sunglasses? In this way you can show how similar you are to the glitterati and fashionistas of this world. Let's face it, they're just like you and me, and probably have crispy pancakes for their dinner, too.

Iced-up with bling bling: After accessorising, you may still feel you've not done enough to tell the world, 'Dammit, I am rich and have no need to shoplift cheese!' And what better way to make this statement than by dripping in gold and diamonds? Or at least looking as if you were? Very few of your friends or 'crew' will be knowledgeable in the world of fine jewellery and will not know a fake piece of zirconia from a lump of kerbstone and so, when you tell them your newest 'diamond'-encrusted MK47 necklace pendant is 94 carats, they won't be in any position to argue with you. (If in any doubt, show it to them in the sunlight, where the dazzle from the stones may blind them and cause temporary hallucinations.) Likewise, there will be no way they will be able to tell your 'horse harness' chunky gold chains are all in fact hollow. You may know that if the gold was any heavier than a fag-paper you'd cause yourself a neck strain, but they should be so impressed with your 'riches', they won't think about it too much.

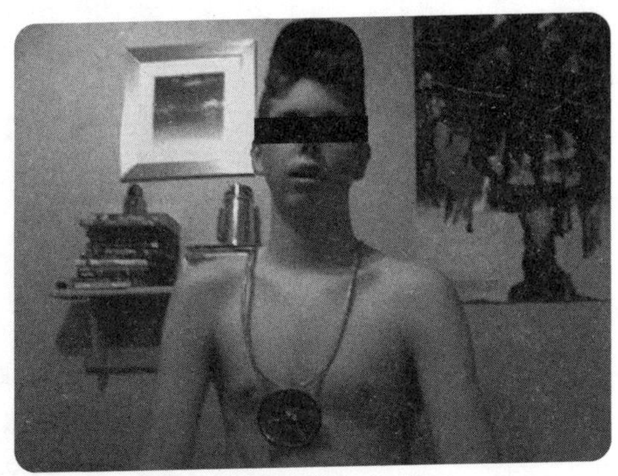

'I'm a new millenium medallion man!'

Gangsta style: The ASBO-seeker should always be aspirational and have their own sense of flair. And, for the less traditional, a totally new fashion experience can be achieved by emulating a 'gangsta' hero of yours. This could range from the new-style rappers who wear furs and 'pimp'-style hats and diamonds to the old-school route of Al Pacino in *Scarface*, with well-cut Italian suits. What is imperative is to keep some trace of your own roots and, say, wear the furs with your track suit or wear the Italian suit with your trainers.

Cinema Etiquette

	DON'T	DO
You are approaching the cinema car park...	Look for a space that is easy to access and will not crowd other parked cars.	Although you are fully able-bodied, park in the nearest disabled space next to the cinema.
You look at the listings and decide to watch 2 films that evening...	Buy an individual ticket for each film.	Buy one ticket and try and sneak into at least one other film, while trying not to get caught by the cinema staff.
Before the film, there is just time to buy a cool beverage and a tasty snack...	Buy a bottled drink that can't be spilled and some chocolate.	Buy a self-service bucket of full-sugar cola (making sure you consume at least a litre before you pay for it) and some nachos that you can crunch on loudly all through the film, before spilling the remainder of your bucket of cola over the floor/seat.

During the trailers, you see that informational film asking patrons to turn off their mobile phones...	Quickly turn your phone off and curse as you forgot to turn it off before you sat down.	Leave your phone on the loudest ringtone setting as you'll probably want to carry out a text message conversation half way through the film.
Half way through the film you feel the need to empty your bladder...	Decide to wait until the end of the film before answering the call of nature.	Immediately get up and disturb the other cinemagoers, spilling your cola and nachos on the floor, before fouling the nearest latrine.

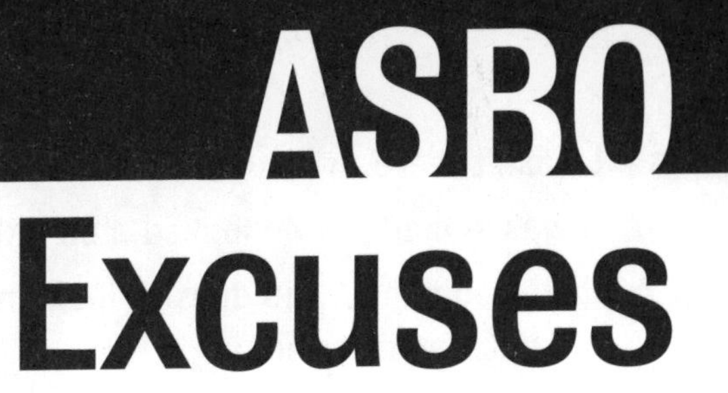
ASBO
Excuses

We might know you want that ASBO, and so might most of your neighbours, but do the authorities know you want one? They do? This is very bad. It is common knowledge that no one ever really gets what they want, so your next step is to convince those who can help you that you really, really don't want an ASBO. To do this you will have to deny all your hard work and tell huge porkies about what you really have been up to.

- **I wasn't there.**
- **It was someone who looked a bit like me.**
- **It was someone who doesn't look anything like me but was dressed up.**
- **I was there but I didn't do anything.**
- **There's no way it was me as I was getting a caution at the time.**
- **I was there and might have done something but I didn't realise I wasn't allowed to.**
- **I was there and did do something but my friends told me to and I didn't realise I didn't have to listen to them.**

'I'm a little hood rat, short and stout...'

- The school hates me.
- The neighbours hate me.
- The shopkeeper hates me.
- My parents hate me.
- The police hate me.
- I'm trying to make this world a better place.
- I have an illness and I can't help myself.
- It's because no one would buy me a Mr Frosty when I was a child.

- I just wanted to see what would happen when I poured the petrol on it.
- It was for a bet. I won the bet in case you're interested.
- It's no worse than what the kids do, and they get away with it, don't they?
- I needed to borrow a tenner and I thought if I borrowed it from Nan's purse without asking I wouldn't have to disturb her too much.
- My friends said everyone was doing it and it wouldn't make any difference if I did it too.
- I mistook the hedgehog for a box of Micro Chips. It's easily done.
- The people in the cemetery are dead so I thought they were finished with the flowers.

'Me mate said that beige tartan is all the rage!'

- I'm trying to save sinners from hell.
- You wouldn't have asked Nelson Mandela why he was starting a petition, now would you?
- I don't like Mondays.
- Sheep have always had it in for me and I wanted to strike back.
- I thought when he said pop round any time he meant even if he wasn't in at the time.
- Likewise, when he said I could borrow the car.
- I was trying to get into the community spirit and start a conga line. At 3 a.m.
- I thought rats were an endangered species and I was starting a breeding programme in the garden.
- I don't see why we have to wear clothes at all times.
- It was all somebody else's fault. Or they did it. Or sumfink.

TOP10

ASBO TV Shows

There's just never anything to watch on TV anymore, and especially nothing relevant to the ASBO-seeker, so here are some ideas it might be fun to try out on TV producers.

Men Women and Children Behaving Badly

Grumpy Old Men

One Man and His Dog – Unmuzzled and Barking

Gardener's World – Super Hedge Special

Buffy the ASBO Slayer – Buffy gets into trouble for her constant staking of vampires and gets herself an ASBO. When called into court she refuses to take that ASBO lying down and calls on all her powers to teach judges a lesson kung fu style.

The ASBO Files – Like the *X- Files* strange and unexplained cases are investigated. The agents suspect alien involvement or strange chemicals added to the water. In the end it turns out that people just like being really annoying.

Last of the Summer Wine – Three old men make a vat of elderbury wine, drink the lot and roam the streets of their small village pulling faces at passers-by, mooning old ladies and growling at children.

Top of the ASBOs – A weekly round-up of the best ASBOs countrywide with all the greatest movers and shakers. Featuring live performances and demonstrations by those who have them.

Watchdog – Not the consumer programme, but a live watch of one very badly behaved dog as the people in the house next door attempt to live their lives without making it bark or snarl.

Question Time – Each week people who have been given an ASBO question the validity of them getting it. In front of a live studio audience, made up of their local neighbourhood.

It's a Knockout – ASBO style – On a Friday night when the pubs kick out, the streets are sprayed with foam and drunks are given costumes and are then encouraged to settle their differences by racing or collecting puzzle pieces instead of actually knocking each other out.

Thunderbirds – Chavettes on a night out are encouraged to let loose their final pretence of being ladylike by engaging in a farting contest.

Spew or Spill? – Contestants view 'pavement pizzas' and guess if they think they are made of vomit or spilled foodstuffs…for big cash prizes!

ASBOs They *Should* Have Got

Getting your ASBO might very well make you a local celebrity, but what of those genuine celebrities and characters and historical figures who might not have been as talented as you are in the ASBO department, but certainly have skated around the same ball park?

Vikki Pollard: Like sand in your knickers, she's only annoying because she's there. Her trademark characteristic is denying she's done anything at all.

The Slaters (*EastEnders*): Girl power. An almost entirely female family of old harpies who seem to enjoy nothing better than a slanging match. They also seem to have an 'easy entry' system in the form of Kat Slater, meaning it is fairly easy for any man to join the gang. As with most ASBO families, there's a quiet one who always seems to have that 'please help me escape from this' look in her eyes. (Although she did end up in court on a murder charge, so perhaps she fits in really.) They subscribe to the old ASBO saying that a row isn't worth having if you don't have it in public.

The Mitchells (*EastEnders*): The male counterparts of the Slaters, this family didn't so much get ASBOs as wipe their arses on them. Any family who keep a lawyer on a permanent payroll have got to be doing something right/wrong.

The Battersbys (*Coronation Street*): A family who are not all related by blood, yet are related by an inability to say anything without screaming the words. Will nick anything not nailed down and seem to spend their entire lives going from the pub to the chip shop and back again. They don't seem to function unless they are in the midst of an ongoing dispute, which can range from Rita in the Cabin to the seventies pop heroes Status Quo. Seriously, you don't get to see the Slaters scrapping with the Nolan Sisters (though we can only dream).

The Family (in *The Hills Have Eyes*): They live in their own commune but refuse not to bother anyone on the grounds that they just can't help themselves and need to feast on human flesh. All very inbred and refuse to mix with outside world. Have general dislike for other people's pets and, if they annoy them, they eat them (probably this is quite unusual but could be the next step up on ASBO evolution).

Victor Meldrew (in *One Foot in the Grave*): No matter what happens to him in his life he isn't happy about it. Is disliked by his neighbours, although he can see only that he is trying to make things better for them.

Rod Hull and Emu: People seemed to forget that there was an arm inside Emu. An arm that was attacking and strangling people. Perhaps you can get away with anything if you also have a puppet.

Henry VIII: Got an ASBO from the pope of his day. Lots of domestic disputes. Fathered many children by lots of different women, most out of wedlock.

Lady Godiva: Didn't much like clothes but did like being looked at.

Robin Hood: Very good at nicking. Lived with his 'crew' in local woodland squat.

Michelangelo: Tagged lots of buildings and painted all over their walls.

The Vikings: Came on a booze-cruise and caused trouble all over the continent.

William the Conqueror: Went to another country and acted as if he owned the place (of course, in his case, he eventually did).

Queen Victoria: Lots of kids. Boundary disputes.

Jesus: Actually did get ASBO and got banned for preaching in temples. Smashed up temple-based businesses. Upset local governments and community leaders.

ASBO Transport

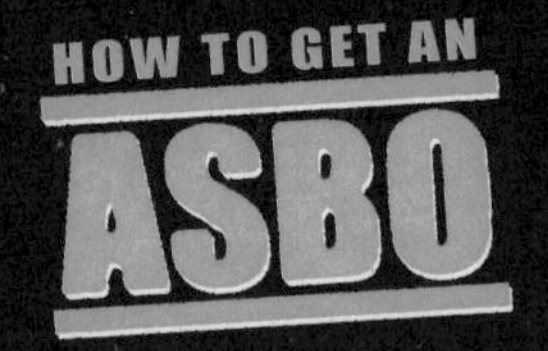

Another way to get an ASBO without really trying hard is via the medium of transport. It's amazing how getting about can get you into all sorts of trouble. You can just be going about your merry way and suddenly you've got an ASBO! Well, hopefully.

Skateboarding

Having first become popular in the seventies, the skateboard has evolved from a pair of roller skates nailed to a plank of wood.

Although the local skate park may be great, for the skater on their way to an ASBO nothing beats street skating, especially in places with lots of seats to jump and handrails to ride. It's not until a skater attempts to ride a handrail down some steps and crashes, crushing his testicles in the process, that he will be caught and given an ASBO forbidding him to skate anywhere except the local park (and to wear a jockstrap!).

Pocket motorbikes

There are times when an avid ASBO-seeker has to carry out the odd errand down to their local corner shop or go round a mate's house to play computer games all day. A problem may arise if they don't have a car (or have been banned from

driving) and they are just too bone idle to get off their arse and walk half a mile.

What can you do when faced with this quandary? See if the local kebab house will pick up twenty fags and some rolling papers for you when they deliver? Con your mate into picking you up in their car? No. The universal 'local' form of transport has arrived: the 'pocket motorbike'. Unlike the skateboard, where an adult is likely to break their neck while learning to ride one, these motorised hairdryers can be driven by anyone who can ride a bike without stabilisers, from a toddler to an adult.

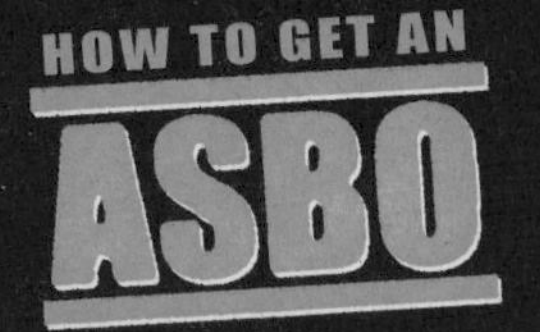

So popular amongst the ASBO community are these miniaturised contraptions that, once one gets one, everyone gets one, usually after they have tried bike-sharing with a friend and realise that two grown adults on one small bike really just isn't possible.

Naturally, proud owners will want to pose with their super-tuned mechanical bumble bees outside the corner shop and race each other. And this is exactly when ASBOs will begin to be handed out!

Shopping trolleys

One commonly held fallacy among ASBO-seekers is that, when you put a pound into the slot to release a shopping trolley at the supermarket, the trolley's yours to take home! However, once you're home with the new 'purchase', its use for anything other than a shopping trolley becomes all too apparent.

Sure, some may turn one upside down in their back yard and use it as a makeshift bunny cage or use one in a modern-art installation, but most are cruelly abandoned on the street like a ginger-haired stepchild.

After an ASBO-seeker has been acquiring a new trolley each time they go shopping, their local area will resemble a shopping-trolley graveyard. And as soon as the mystery source of this glut of trolleys is found, an ASBO is slapped on, which limits you to hand baskets when shopping!

Modded cars

As you can see, there are many forms of transport that can get you an ASBO, but nothing beats the modified car and the culture that surrounds it. For the unsuspecting or just plain dumb, the 'Barry'd Up' automobile can get you an ASBO faster than any other method of transport.

This bastion of chav culture is all about bolting illegal crap on to your ten-year-old car, devaluing it to a point where it's virtually worthless, then parading it in front of other chavs. There are a number of 'mods' that a chav can make to their

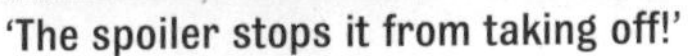

'The spoiler stops it from taking off!'

ASBO-mobile that can make them illegal for road use in one fell swoop. For example, a large, chrome baked-bean-can exhaust that makes a small car louder than a 747 jumbo jet, a dazzling array of blue neon lights that can blind oncoming drivers or a number plate in a completely unintelligible font.

If this is not bad enough, once you have an ASBO-mobile, the thing to do is go on a 'cruise'. This is a euphemism for like-minded illegal car drivers to meet up in an out-of-town retail park and race their machines. To the delight of the police, these 'cruises' are often advertised and for them is a chance to dish out ASBOs on a mass scale!

'It's me pride and joy, innit?'

There we have it. If it has wheels, an avid ASBO-seeker can almost certainly use it to get where they are going fast – acquiring an ASBO.

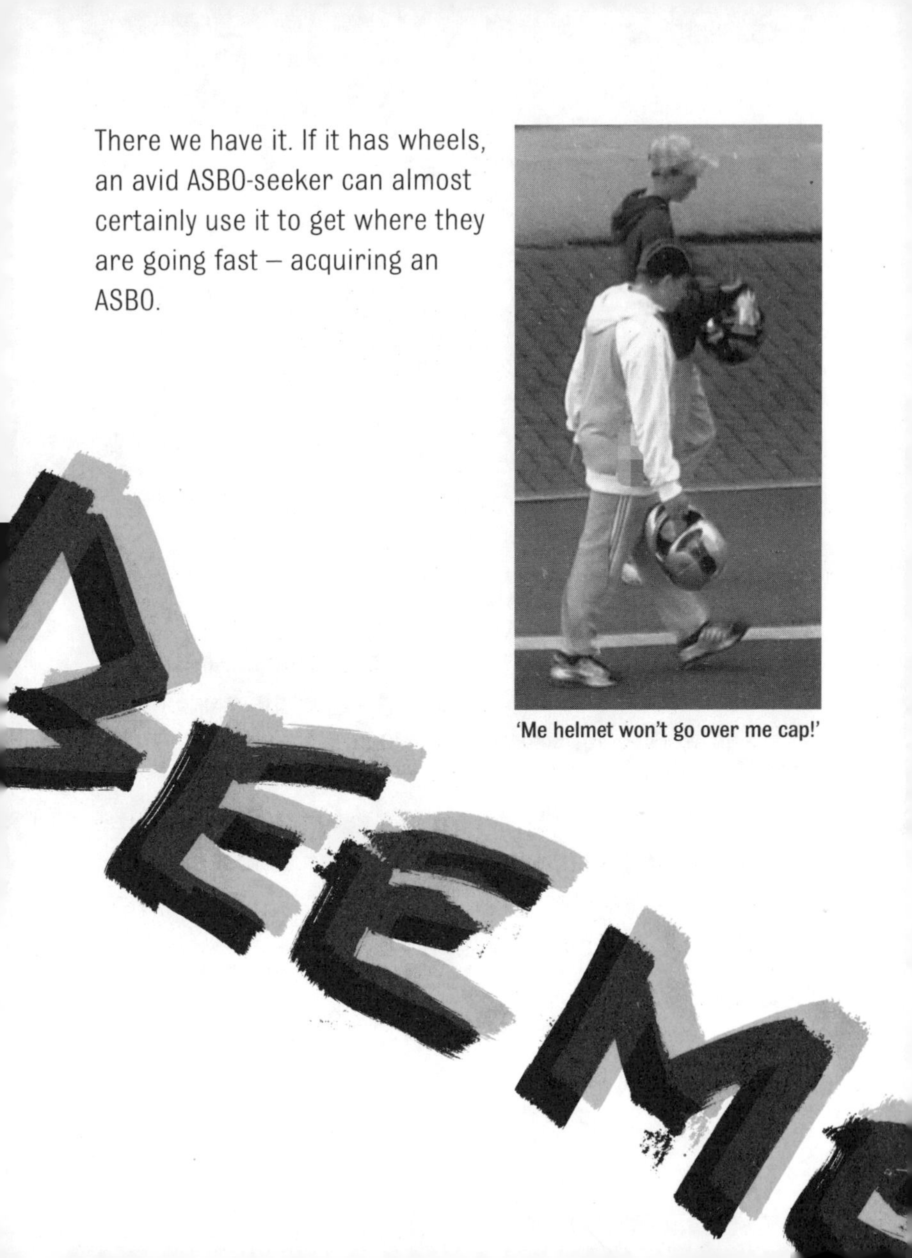

'Me helmet won't go over me cap!'

TOP 10

Most ASBO Animals

1. **Wasps** – Unlike bees they refuse to serve a purpose and make anything other than a nuisance of themselves.

2. **Lions** – The male of the species thinks he is tough and scary but in reality he just lies about sleeping and waiting for his missus to bring him dinner.

3. **Elephants** – Stubborn and set in their ways but try arguing with one and you realise its just easier to let them have their own way as they never forget and always bear a grudge.

4. **Tigers** – See lions. But with added bling.

5 **Rattlesnakes** – Have a nasty sting in their tails but spend most of their time just TELLING you about it.

6 **Cockerels** – Have a lovely habit of thinking everyone is interested in what they have to say. Even though they only ever inform us it is morning.

7 **Hamsters** – Sleep all day then spend all night eating, drinking and playing with their wheels.

8 **Hyenas** – Rather than doing their own shopping and cooking, they wait for another animal to do it then nick it off them. And giggle with their mates about it.

9 **Mynah birds** – Can imitate human speech and learn to communicate, but they mainly use this talent to shout 'bollocks' when the local vicar comes to visit.

10 **Bears** – Think they can do what they like and really lose their temper if they have any restrictions placed on them.

The Opposite of ASBO

Well, as we've seen, there are lots of good ways to get an ASBO. There are also lots of things that will never get you an ASBO, so don't even waste your time. Here, to make things a little more black and white, are things not to bother with:

- **going to church on a Sunday (unless it is to shout, 'I am Lucifer incarnate!' after the hymns);**
- **helping an elderly lady home with her shopping;**
- **assisting a blind person across a busy road;**
- **volunteering at a local charity shop;**
- **feeding local wildlife (unless it encourages rats and assorted vermin to establish a stronghold in your back garden);**
- **becoming a prison visitor (unless it is to pick up tips and career advice);**
- **volunteering to help at the hospital (unless it is to get a peek at semi-dressed nurses);**
- **baking cakes to sell at a fête;**

- walking a neighbour's dog;
- taking in a parcel for your next-door neighbour;
- watering the tomato plants in a neighbour's greenhouse;
- buying a copy of the *Big Issue*;
- visiting your gran and her friends at the old folks' home;
- reporting a drug dealer to the police;
- spending time at the library (unless it is so that you can meticulously study the parking laws and quote them on the next Post-it note that you stick on the windscreen of a parking offender);
- teaching your nephew about classical music (unless you stick it on your stereo at 38 decibels);
- offering to help out at your local youth club.

When Old Gits Go Bad

Getting an ASBO is a tough business and there's nothing like age and experience to help you get one. If we look to the more mature members of our community, they often have a lot to teach us about being annoying.

When you think of an ASBO-seeker, the image of a teenage chav springs to mind. However, there is a new group of ASBO-seekers who are taking on the teenage tearaways at their own game: the feral pensioner. When good OAPs go bad, they can unleash a reign of terror over a neighbourhood that can have them receiving their first ASBO before you can say 'vigilante'.

Unlike teenage chavs, old gits (and it is almost always men) do not aspire to having an ASBO and are disgusted when they receive one for their antisocial behaviour. Most OAP ASBO-seekers have the same psychological profile. During their working years, their job was their life. Their work, no matter how mundane, defined them and kept them alive. When they finally retire, the hole left in their life can be similar to that of a drug addict kicking a heroin habit.

Unlike most pensioners who use their new abundance of leisure time to take up new hobbies, travel the world or just kick back and take it easy, the OAP ASBO-seeker becomes fixated with antisocial behaviour and minor social menaces. Most people don't even know these problems exist in society or are too busy getting on with their lives to care about them. The study of this sociological phenomenon has its own scholastic term: 'gitology'. Here we present our guide for aspiring grumpy old gits and pissed-off pensioners to get that coveted ASBO.

Noise nuisance

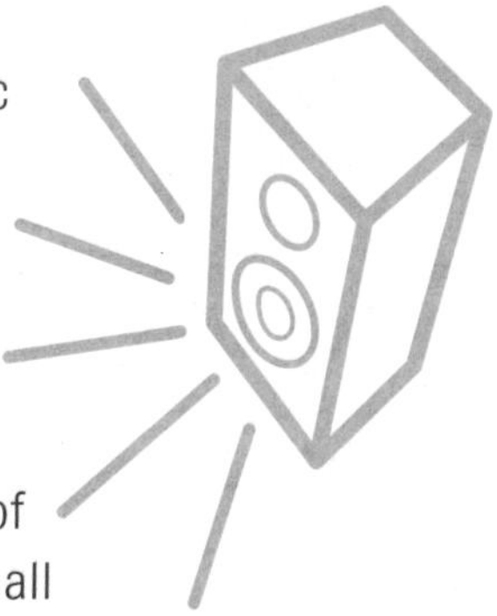

Unlike the noisy chav who plays music at 4 a.m., the OAP ASBO-seeker is the antithesis of the noisy neighbour. Although their neighbour may be as quiet as church mice, the OAP ASBO-seeker will be convinced that their neighbour is destroying their quality of life with intolerable noise pollution at all times of the day and night. The old git's first port of call will be the local authority, in the hope of getting a noise-abatement order for their neighbours. Naturally, said old git will say that their neighbours must have seen the council employees coming to their house and now they are being quiet, when they don't hear anything untoward. This is when the grumpy old sod will spend thousands of pounds sound-proofing their home as protection against their quiet neighbour.

They will also buy sophisticated audio equipment to record the perceived noise nuisance from next door (which they won't bother to learn how to use properly so all the 'evidence' will be totally useless anyway), in the hope of finally getting them prosecuted or evicted.

Boundary disputes

It is a well-known fallacy held by OAP ASBO-seekers that, if you have lived in your house longer than your neighbours, then they have no boundary rights whatsoever. Just like chavs, grumpy old bastards are never happier than when they have an enemy to fight. If you are unlucky enough to move in next to an OAP ASBO-seeker, you may become his enemy if you ever want to put up a new fence or you have children or, worst of all, one or more cats!

Once you've moved in you may find that your OAP ASBO-seeker will be quite a private individual and, when you do talk to them, you will find them to be quite pleasant. It's only when you approach them about replacing the 'chicken wire and scrap wood' fence that it says on your deeds is your legal responsibility to keep in good repair, that your OAP neighbour will show his true ASBO colours! The torrent of abuse you may receive could be something like this:

'I've been here forty f**kin' years, it's my f**kin' fence, I don't care what it says on your f**kin' deeds, you f**kin' touch it and I'll f**kin' 'ave you! I'll burn your f**kin' house down, with your f**kin' kids in it!'

If you are not put off by such threats, you will have to prepare yourself for the geriatric shit storm that could be about to come your way. You will naturally find that, the first time you try to erect a new fence, the grumpy old sod next door will try to cut it down with a saw or an angle grinder as soon as you go out. Don't be perturbed, though: eventually he'll get the message that the new fence is here to stay.

Mobility karts

If you are a pensioner and find it difficult to get around, a mobility kart can make all the difference to your life, giving you back your freedom and independence. However, in the hands of an OAP ASBO-seeker these vehicles can become a true menace.

Nice ride

When a grumpy old sod gets their first mobility kart, one of their first acts of madness will be to assume that an electric-powered kart with a top speed of 15 m.p.h. is the same as a car. They will hold up the whole town by driving their geriatric milk float in the centre of the left-hand lane from their house on the outskirts, down to the town centre and back. Completely oblivious of the congestion chaos and the hair-raising near-misses left in their wake, our mobile pensioner will already be on their way to an ASBO.

Once the OAP ASBO-seeker has been taken off the road and put back on the pavement, the grumpy old sod will then turn their wrath on pedestrians. Blessed with the lovely attitude that you command respect rather than earn it if you are over 65, the old git will ride the pavements thinking that all pedestrians should get out of their way immediately, like Moses parting the Red

Sea (this is where the extra-loud air-horn upgrade on the mobility kart comes in handy). Heaven help the pedestrian who doesn't get out of their way in time. If the OAP ASBO-seeker does manage to injure a pedestrian, they will of course claim that the pedestrian deliberately tried to damage their mobility kart and announce they are going to sue them!

Dog shit and pavements

As we said earlier, it's the small things that the OAP ASBO-seeker gets obsessed with. Sure, dog shit and uneven paving slabs are a nuisance, but the average person doesn't give much thought to them. For our OAP ASBO-seeker, these seemingly inconsequential problems can become the focus of a full-time campaign. It may all start with numerous ill-informed letters of complaint to the local paper. On the following pages are a couple of examples. See if you can spot similar letters in your local rag.

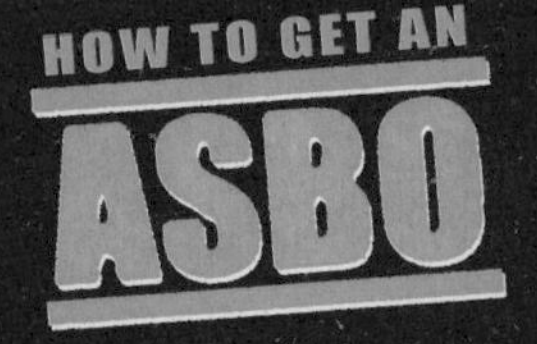

First the dog-shite rant!

Dear Sir

I am writing to you and your readers to inform you about the alarming rise in the amount of dog excreta on the pavement of Nowhere Close and the surrounding Gitville area. At dawn every morning I conduct my own excrement survey and can reveal that the number of 'dogs' eggs' on our pavements has increased almost 20% in the last quarter. If the council do not do something to stop irresponsible dog owners from allowing their pets to do plop-plops on the pavements of our town, our streets will soon become one giant dog toilet! Perhaps rather than spending money on unessential frivolities like playgrounds and public toilets, the council should be ploughing more of our hard-earned council tax monies into research on why canine bottom excretion seems to be on the rise.

Yours sincerely

Major Meddlesome-Ratbag (Retired)
21 Nowhere Close
Gitville

And now the less popular paving slabs example rant!

Dear Sir

I am writing to you and your readers to inform you about the shocking state of the pavements in Nowhere Close and all across Gitville. In my close alone, I counted 17 paving slabs that were either unlevelled or had an edge protruding out of the surface by more than a quarter of an inch. These Mount Everest-style paving slabs are a health hazard. Not only do I get an extremely bumpy ride in my mobility kart, a child could trip on one and have an eye out or something! I should imagine if you are a young person who is in the prime of their life and watch where they are going it is easy to avoid taking a tumble, but as a pensioner who has to remain vigilant against street crime at every minute of her waking life, it is harder to do. Not that I expect you are all that bothered even though it's people like me that keep you in a job.

Yours sincerely

Mrs Grumpy Old-Bat
(address supplied)

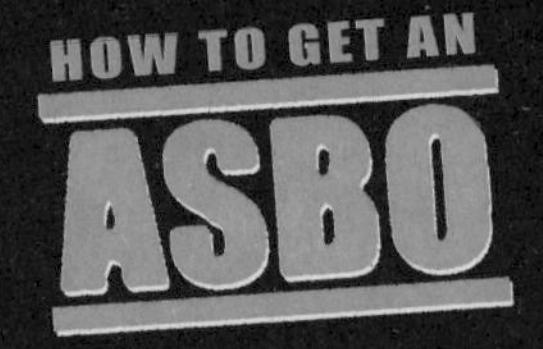

The Queen's highway

For some reason, OAP ASBO-seekers can't resist the lure of becoming unpaid traffic wardens. Cars parked on double yellow lines, vehicles with no road tax, vans loading and unloading at the wrong time of day – just about any road-traffic violation can become the bugbear of the grumpy old git. One thing in particular, though, can grab their attention like no other: road tax.

The first day of the month is always bliss for the road-traffic-obsessed OAP ASBO-seeker. They will spend the day touring their local neighbourhood looking for cars where the road tax expired the day before. If they find one, they will take a sadistic pleasure in ringing the local authority to report the vehicle. In some cases, like a deranged serial killer, they will stay at the location until the local authority personnel arrive either to clamp or remove the vehicle to the pound, to get that sense of closure.

The bible of the road-traffic OAP ASBO-seeker is of course the Highway Code. Not only will they know the law inside and out, they will also know all the obscure bylaws that apply to their area. When a grumpy old sod's reign of terror over their local neighbourhood regarding car tax and parking on double yellow lines has made almost all residents live in fear of the zero-tolerance old git and stay 100 per cent on the right side of the law, they may then embark on what they think of as an essential road-safety campaign of reporting people who break even the most minor parking laws. This is when our grumpy old sod unknowingly starts their journey to ASBO land!

So, as you can see, it's not just chavs that can be antisocial. The lovely old granddad who lives in your road could easily become a surprise owner of an ASBO!

TOP 10

ASBO FoodStuffs

Not the food that fuels the ASBO-seeker but foods that are, in themselves a bit ASBO.

1. **Nachos** – Who thought these would be a good idea as a cinema snack? Smelly and impossible to eat without crunching.

2. **Chips with salt and vinegar** – Anyone smelling these wants to eat them even though they can't/shouldn't/won't or feels very sick at the combination of grease and acidity.

3. **Popcorn** – See Nachos. But a bit cheaper and also easier to throw at people.

4. **Spaghetti bolognese** – Very few people seem to know how to eat it properly and when you get it all over your shirt (as you invariably will) it stains within seconds.

⑤ **Pomegranates** – A fruit made mainly of seeds. Almost totally pointless. (Although seeds are often fun to flick at passers-by.)

⑥ **Milkshakes** – For those who like people to know when they are drinking. Thick milkshakes just get noisier and more annoying as they get to the end.

⑦ **Bubblegum** – If you're not blowing bubbles with it, you're leaving it on the pavement where it can ruin someone's shoes. Doesn't make you less hungry, doesn't even refresh your breath.

⑧ **Candy floss** – Even more pointless than bubblegum and less satisfying. The only filling you will get is from your dentist.

⑨ **Fizzy drinks** – So eager to be consumed they leap straight from the bottle/can and all over your clothes as soon as you begin to open them. The small amount you have left in the bottom after you have mopped yourself down will ironically then be flat.

⑩ **Ice Cream and Lollies** – Give either of these to a small child and they will drip them all over benches, phone boxes, post boxes and anything people have to use. Or else the kids will generously drop them on the floor so as they can attract a ton of wasps or ants or both.

ASBO Quiz: Are You ASBO Enough?

Before you take that last plunge into ASBO and complete your quest for the glittering prize, it's as well to see if you are ready for its trials or if you could go back and do a bit more work to get yourself up to standard. To help with this, we have compiled a handy quiz to see what you have learned and just how irritating you are. And, although being devious and sneaky is usually an attribute that is useful to ASBO-seekers, we encourage you, just for once, not to cheat.

Question 1

After narrowly avoiding a brawl after leaving a nightclub, you decide to return home. Which of these do you do?

A. Say goodbye to your friends. When home, make yourself a hot milky drink and retire to bed for a little reading to unwind, before you fall asleep.

B. Invite your friends and the neighbourhood bikes back to your house for a public broadcast of your favourite drum-and-bass albums to be accompanied by copious imbibing of white cider. Finally you fall unconscious, face down in your hallway around 6 a.m. in a stupor after throwing up on your cat/partner/Playstation.

Question 2

You are rudely awoken from your peaceful slumber after last night's festivities by an irate neighbour who complains that he did not get a wink of sleep during the night. Which of these do you do?

A. Apologise profusely, clearly stating that what happened the night before will never happen again and your respected neighbour can be guaranteed a peaceful night's sleep from now on.

B. Wipe the sick from your hair, before launching into a tirade of insults, referencing your neighbour's mother's sexuality in the crudest manner possible.

Question 3

Perhaps today is a good day and you are feeling fine. You wake feeling refreshed and ready to greet the day. This is very different from the 'mouth like used cat litter and face hit with the shovel' feeling you are used to. To celebrate, you decide to have some cereal. There is no milk in the house. What do you do?

A. Pull on the jogging trousers that you wear for just such morning opportunities as this and take some good healthy exercise on the way to the convenience store, where the proprietor greets you with a cheery hello.

B. Find some trousers at the side of the bed that may or may not belong to you, wipe off the worst of the hair of the mongrel dog that had been using them as a bed and stagger the 200 yards to the corner shop, where the owner watches you like a hawk, with his finger hovering over the speed-dial to the police station.

Question 4

Oh, dear! In your hurry it seems you have forgotten to bring any money with you! Do you ...?

A. Explain your predicament to the shopkeeper, hoping he will feel in a generous mood and allow you to take the milk and drop the money in later. Of course, if this isn't acceptable you can always go home and get some money – it isn't the end of the world.

B. When your attempt at establishing a mate at the corner shop is refused, leave the shop shouting at the injustice of it all as you go.

Question 5

On your way back home you chance across a lost mobile telephone. Which do you do?

A. Find a number in the phone that you can use to trace the owner to inform them of their loss and tell them where they can collect it from. You feel a warm glow inside because you have been so much help.

B. Ignore it. If you hand it in, people might think you'd nicked it, right?

Question 6

Sadly you seem to be out of work at the moment, so today you will have to visit the jobcentre. How do you feel about this?

A. A bit disheartened. Being out of work is soul-destroying, but going to the jobcentre is a step in the right direction. You never know what's around the corner and today might just be the day you find something good.

B. Don't really care one way or another. Everyone you know is out of work and it's good to go to the jobcentre to catch up with your mates. Although you never know what's around the corner and you hope today is not the day that someone's grassed you up for selling dodgy fags in the pub.

Question 7

On the way home from the jobcentre you see some local kids spraying graffiti on the side of a house. Do you …?

A. Give them a lecture about having respect for other people's property. Explain to them that there are lots more productive ways they could use their time, and try to make them promise not to do it again. Be nice, though: they are only kids and there's no point being too threatening

B. Laugh at them and remember when you were younger and did the same sort of tricks. Then notice it is your house they are spraying and try to attack them and teach them a lesson they won't forget (if only you could catch them). Be as civil as you can be while talking to them: they are only kids and so are in far better fighting form than you are.

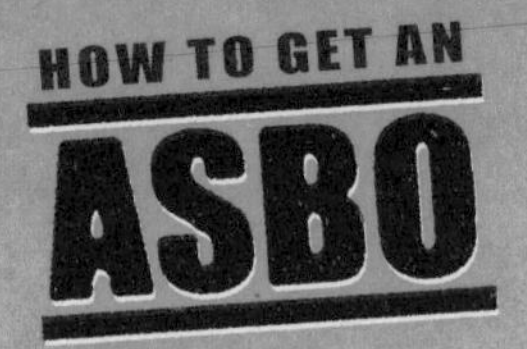

Question 8

Ouch! The local kids didn't appreciate your advice much and seem to have given you a bit of a pasting. Probably best to get that looked at in casualty. So what do you do when you arrive there?

A. Check yourself in at the desk. Explain what has happened to you and wait patiently for your turn to be seen. You're not really that bad compared with some other patients, and the poor staff seem to be overrun.

B. Fling yourself at the check-in desk. Wail about the pain and tell anyone who will listen how you were set upon by fifteen local gangsters who were all fully armed, and then you had to drag yourself to casualty because no one called a much-needed ambulance for you. When the receptionist tells you how long your wait will be, cause a huge ruckus until the police are called and you get sent home with a strip of Elastoplast and an aspirin.

Question 9

After all the day's excitement, you decide to have a relaxing evening at home. What are your plans?

A. Ring for a takeaway. Down to the off-licence for a bottle of wine. Perhaps a walk to the video shop to get out one of the latest releases. Come home and enjoy some good company (partner and kids or perhaps some like-minded friends). Ah, perfect!

B. Call up some mates and get them to bring beer and a porn DVD and watch it loudly till midnight. Ah, bliss!

Question 10

An early night will do you good. What's the routine you always follow before bed?

A. Make sure all appliances are turned off. Check if you've locked the door. Put the cat out. Look in on your sleeping cherubic children and then brush your teeth and slip into bed.

B. Make sure all fags are smoked (it's not good to be wasteful). Pop outside to make sure the dog is chained up in such a way that will encourage it to bark all night. Look in on your kids and, even if they're not at home, lock the door so they can't get in and will have to bang loudly when they finally arrive home at 2 a.m. Clean the worst of the fur off your tongue, swig some flat beer as a nightcap and crash out on the sofa.

Results

Mostly As

Have you learned nothing? You almost seem to be going out of your way to try to be a useful and productive member of society! You don't get an ASBO for being a decent upstanding citizen. Please go back to the beginning of the book and start again. Tsk, tsk! There's just no helping some people.

Mostly Bs

Congratulations! You have learned what you need to do and are doing it to a high standard. If you don't already have an ASBO, then one is surely just around the corner, or there is no justice in the world. (Actually, the way you behave, you'd better hope there isn't too much justice in the world or you might find yourself in choky soon as well.)

TOP 10 ASBO Films

When you're not out there seeking your ASBO what better way to entertain yourself than a good film? Here are our suggestions for films that could be ASBO'd up a bit.

1. ***Titanic*** – Rose tries to throw herself off the ship. In the ASBO version she would have been sick all over the side of the boat, she wouldn't have thanked Jack for rescuing her, and her mother would have taken legal action against him for touching her daughter in an inappropriate fashion.

2. ***Jurassic Park*** – The owner of the park gets served with an ASBO stating that he has to keep all carnivorous dinosaurs muzzled, and provide Poop Scoop bins for the larger herbivores.

3. ***The Contant Gardener*** – All that constant gardening is bloody annoying to his neighbours.

4. ***Independence Day*** – In the ASBO version the aliens' spaceship is clamped and they are served with an ASBO mere minutes after entering our atmosphere. When this ASBO is broken the United Nations shows their planetary strength by sending

them a very strongly worded letter and the Aliens realise our planet is no fun and go home.

5 ***Superman*** – When saving the world time after time, he does often cause a lot of damage to property. Several citizens of Metropolis get together and serve him with a CCJ that will affect his ability to buy pants from a catalogue for years to come.

6 ***Braveheart*** – In the ASBO version Wallace gets served with an ASBO for stirring up public unrest, which he then takes to the pub to show his mates and the next time he meets the English he tells them to 'F**k off' and lifts his kilt at them.

7 ***The Omen*** – A little boy has the mark of the devil. And a crew-cut and Crazy Frog T-Shirt. People believe he might well be the anti-Christ until they look around the neighbourhood and see another 17 just like him.

8 ***The Ring*** – Nothing much happens as the last person who got it out didn't bring it back to the video shop.

9 ***Pirates of the Caribbean*** – Not so much high seas and swashbuckling as 'It only come out daaahn the pictures this week' and 'I'll do ya three for a tenner' type action.

10 ***King Kong*** – A large, hairy, shirtless primate terrorises a neighbourhood, grunting and leering at women. Sounds alright as it is.

What to Do With Your ASBO

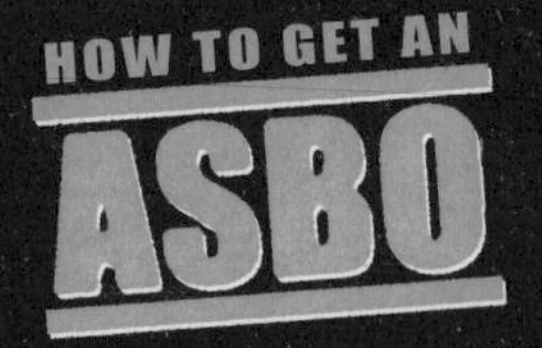

OK, so you've followed the advice to the letter and got yourself a bright, shiny, new ASBO. But, as with an exam certificate or a wedding certificate (not that you'll have either of those things, probably), it's up to you to make it worth more than just a piece of paper. It's up to you to make it count. What can you do with it now?

1. Place the letters ASBO after your name every time you have to write/sign/tag anything. Much like the letters PhD or Hons, your credentials will not fail to impress people.

2. Make sure everyone knows you have one by contacting the local press. This will assure that you reach a decent level of local celebrity, but will unfortunately mean that everyone who knows and hates you will be just dying for you to break the conditions so they can grass you up.

3. Sit in the pub and pretend that you 'don't wanna talk about it', but bring it into every part of the conversation and even whip it from your pocket and show it to people at every opportunity.

4. Make copies of it and tear one of them up in the pub now and again to show everyone just how much you don't care about it. (Don't tear the real one up, or else you might get into trouble and you want an ASBO, not a prison sentence. Anyway, you'll need the original to make more copies from.)

5. If someone hard says something bad to you, you can ignore them and not look like a total chicken by saying, 'I'd lay 'im out but I can't 'cos of me ASBO.'

6. Use it to impress local gullible chicks or posh birds who want a bad-lad boyfriend to annoy their parents with.

7. If you are an old git, write to your local paper/your PM/the Queen telling them of the injustice of your getting such a thing for working for the good of the community and that 'you didn't fight in a war to be treated like this'.

8. Use it as an excuse not to do anything you don't want to do any more due to being 'depressed' over getting it – sort of like, 'Our Shayne can't do no manual labour. He's still too depressed over that ASBO and it affects his strength.'

9. Tell everyone that, now you have an ASBO, you have had your passport taken away and other countries refuse to let you in, because you might be a danger to their society and that's why you're not going on holiday.

10. If you do happen to have any relatives not bursting with pride about your ASBO, tell them this is a totally different thing and actually stands for Award for Shining, Bright Obedience and you got it for services to street football and helping local shopkeepers.

11. Take your ASBO on a tour of local schools and warn kids of the dangers of ASBO culture: 12–14-year-olds will hero-worship anyone and should be impressed by your exploits.

12. If you're not too into the ASBO lifestyle, go to your local church and find Jesus. There's nothing better to them than a repenting sinner.

13. If you can write, write your memoirs. Pretend to be a cockney and make up lots of stuff about your gangland exploits and you're guaranteed a bestseller!

14. If you have a friend who also has an ASBO, why not partake in a game of ASBO top trumps, to see whose ASBO is the better one?

15. Finally, and most importantly, just relax, secure in the knowledge that your ASBO credentials have been established and you have proved you're up there in the bad-lad/lass league and, more importantly, you have evidence to prove this. Sure, you could go to jail and people might be more impressed, but with an ASBO you get to enjoy the benefits of seeing people who know that 'you da man'.

Index